PENNSYLVANIA MADE

Homegrown Products by Local Craftsmen, Artisans, and Purveyors

Bernadette Sukley

Globe Pequot

Guilford, Connecticut

All the information in this guidebook is subject to change. We recommend you call ahead to obtain current information before traveling.

Globe Pequot

An imprint of Rowman & Littlefield

Distributed by NATIONAL BOOK NETWORK

British Library Cataloguing in Publication Information Available

Library of Congress Cataloging-in-Publication Data Available

ISBN 978-1-4930-1326-5 (paperback)
ISBN 978-1-4930-1327-2 (e-book)

∞™ The paper used in this publication meets the minimum requirements of American National Standard for Information Sciences—Permanence of Paper for Printed Library Materials, ANSI/NISO Z39.48-1992.

Introduction

Pennsylvania has a remarkable history of innovation, entrepreneurship, quality craftsmanship, manufacturing, and good old-fashioned guts. Ingenuity and free-thinking ideas have always been keys to success in the Keystone State. Historically famous for covered bridges, steam engines, steel, and pretzels, Pennsylvania is seeing a resurgence of old businesses and a revival of arts that were disappearing. New companies established by artisans young and old are flourishing. Visit and purchase from these Pennsylvanians to help support them and preserve history.

The 250 entries in this book are only the tip of the iceberg—the Pennsylvania iceberg—they are by no means an exhaustive collection of the crafts, companies, people, and history representative of Pennsylvania. The good news is that there are new businesses popping up every day, so there's always something new to discover. The bad news is that many of these enterprises are struggling from misrepresentation, burdensome regulations, and unfair competition from overseas. Some may be gone next year. I encourage you to discover, learn, and enjoy everything Pennsylvanian as soon as you can—you won't want to miss any of it.

How to Use This Book

Organized by county, the entries in this book discuss the people behind the product, a little bit of local history, where their ideas came from or how they started, and what makes the establishment special and unique. Establishments are listed alphabetically under each county heading. You will find information on a wide assortment of places, from ceramics to clothing, ice cream to spirits, fishing lures to stained glass creations.

Contents by Type

Contents by County

Acknowledgments

A huge thanks to my cheerleader, friend, and promoter of all things Pennsylvania made, Karey Poniktera. I wish I could buy you one of everything in this book!

To my children (all Pennsylvania made, thank you very much), Bernadette Marie, Rich, Celeste, and Steven, who never let me forget what matters most in this world—food, family, and fun. And to my husband Marty, who is the happiest on a Pennsylvania stream, in a Pennsylvania forest, or on top of a Pennsylvania mountain. You're a big part of the reason why I love this state so much.

And to all the purveyors included in this book, thank you for sharing your stories. Because of you and the love of what you do, many people will be inspired to discover and be a part of all of the good things about Pennsylvania. You're in my heart.

Good Intent Farm, FURNITURE, 270 Bakers Watering Trough Rd., East Berlin 17316; (717) 259-5787; andy@goodintentfarm.com; goodintentfarm.com. Andy Grimes is the person to help you with your home. Need a place to sit, rest a lamp, or store dishes? If its woodworking and furniture, he's your man, well, furniture maker. Good Intent Farm's specialty is primitive-style and Shaker furniture. The lines are simple and harken back to a time when function outweighed embellishment. A subset of the Quakers, the Shakers settled in Pennsylvania in the 1700s and incorporated the principles of honesty, utility, and simplicity in furniture, crafts, and textiles. They were renowned for their minimalist design and high quality. Rejecting excessive ornament, Shaker furniture demonstrates symmetry and proportion. Most pieces were originally painted or stained, both to protect the wood and to make it more attractive. Colors were strictly regulated and limited to muted tones of blue, green, red, and yellow. Good Intent Farm furniture has the look of age and gentle wear, as if it had been rescued from a Shaker home. Andy has managed to age and distress his furniture without compromising the integrity of the wood. His primitive pieces are aged, without the feebleness of an antique. Contact Andy prior to your visit to check his availability and get directions. Be sure to use "directions" in the subject line of your email.

Oyler's Organic Farms, FARMS, 400 Pleasant Valley Rd., Biglerville 17307; (717) 677-8411; oylersorganicfarms.com. Market hours are Jan through Aug and Dec, Tues through Fri, 10 a.m. to 6 p.m. and Sat, 9 a.m. to 4 p.m.; Sept through Nov, Tues through Fri, 10 a.m. to 6 p.m., Sat, 9 a.m. to 4 p.m., and Sun, noon to 4 p.m. Oyler's Organic Farms is a family farm consisting of husband and wife team Bill and Mary Ann Oyler and their grown children, Sara, Jacob, and Katrina. Bill is the fifth generation to farm the same land, so he truly has the heart of a farmer. It helps that he has farmed his entire life. But he's also a graduate of Gettysburg College with a degree in Business Administration. When Bill isn't knee deep in produce, he's reading a book, magazine, newspaper, or searching the Internet for new ideas to incorporate into the farm. Mary Ann grew up on a dairy farm and has since "migrated" into love of the fruit industry. It was motivated, in part, by her marriage in 1984 to Bill, who's an agri-geek (nerdy farmers are trending these days). Mary Ann is a graduate of Indiana University of Pennsylvania with a degree in Consumer Sciences, so it's no surprise she's a fan of canning her farm's produce. Oldest daughter, Sara, is Penn State Proud and has a degree in Agroecology, a field of study that combines ecology with agricultural production systems. The idea is to sustain the land, the farm, and the people. Oyler's offers organic apples, cider, and organic peaches as well as seasonal produce. They also have eggs, free-range chicken, turkey, pork, and grass-fed beef.

Allegheny

The Church Brew Works, BREWERY, 3525 Liberty Ave., Pittsburgh, 15201; (412) 688-8200; churchbrew.com. Open Sun, 11:30 a.m. to 9 p.m.; Mon through Thurs, 11:30 a.m. to 11 p.m.; Fri and Sat, 11:30 a.m. to midnight. A brewery in a church? Yep. From the sublime to the pilsner-licious, Church Brew Works makes beer in an unrepentant fashion. Formerly St. John the Baptist Church, the parish once served an exploding immigrant population of Irish, Polish, and German men and women who came to work in the working man's city. A fire, flood, The Great Depression, two world wars, and a failing steel industry took their toll on the community and the parish. Dwindling resources and attendance forced the school to close in the 1970s, and the church finally closed in 1993. The property was bought and reopened as a brewery—it had all the right parts for a place to handcraft beer and ales. First, it had one huge, lofty ceiling to accommodate tall steel and copper brewing tanks. Second, the side aisles were ideally suited for the long bars needed for tastings. Once the pews were removed, the space opened to allow for tables and patrons—Church Brew Works offers a full menu, not your typical brewpub fare. Lastly, there was plenty of storage in the basement. Although the church-to-brewery transition may seem a bit blasphemous to some, there's always a bartender willing to listen to your confession and a heavenly brew to help you solve the world's problems. Hint: Try their Pipe Organ Pale Ale—brewed with American hops, it's crisp, without regrets or bitterness.

Heinz History Center, FOOD/HISTORY, 1212 Smallman St., Pittsburgh 15222; (412) 454-6000; heinzhistorycenter.org. Visiting hours are Mon through Fri, 10 a.m. to 5 p.m. In 1896 H.J. Heinz was inspired by an ad he saw that read, "21 Styles of Shoes." Using what he considered to be a lucky number, he developed the slogan, Heinz57, and opened a food processing plant in Sharpsburg (5 miles northeast of Pittsburgh). Despite the fact that the company offered more than 60 different products, the "57 varieties" moniker stuck. Heinz essentially spiced up a very bland American diet. He insisted on using clear bottles so people could see the food inside. In 1871, he introduced bottled ketchup. Many farmers were already selling the sweet, vinegary tomato sauce, but Heinz was able to market the condiment as a "relief to women" because it saved them the time and labor of making it themselves. Heinz was also able to make inroads into sanitary bottling practices to reduce bacterial contamination—even going as far as to have employees who handled food receive weekly manicures. But the emphasis was on cleanliness, not pretty hands. Today, the company makes mustard, vinegar, relish, steak sauce, and pickles. It has also acquired food product lines such as pet foods, tuna, cookies, and baby food. But ketchup is by far its best-known food item. Heinz sells 650 million bottles of ketchup each year. Explore the company's rich foodie history through the center's many events held throughout the year. Check the website for dates and details.

Hunt Stained Glass Studios, GLASS, 1756 West Carson St., Pittsburgh, 15219; (412) 391-1796; huntsgpgh@gmail.com; huntstainedglass.com. For individual and group tours, please contact prior to date of visit. The Henry Hunt Studio is one of the largest and oldest stained glass facilities in Pennsylvania. Henry was born in England in 1867 and trained with his father as a stained glass apprentice. He immigrated to Boston in the late 19th century and began working for Leake & Greene (self-proclaimed decorators) in the mid-1880s. While there, Henry created the Thaw Memorial *reredos* (a screen or decoration behind a church altar) for H. H. Richardson's Emmanuel Episcopal Church in what was then Allegheny City. In 1906, Henry founded his own studio, called Henry Hunt Studio. He chose Pittsburgh's West End to set up shop and the same studio is still in operation today as Hunt Stained Glass Studios. Henry's children, George, James, Franklin, and Marianne, apprenticed under their father and expanded the business, bringing in noted stained glass artists such as Helen Carew Hickman, Charles Morris, and Roy Calligan. James (Jimmy) became the studio's head foreman. George became involved in the professional stained glass community, presiding as president of the prestigious Stained Glass Association of America for several years. During this time, the studio's name changed to Hunt Stained Glass Studios, and George acquired Aurora Stained Glass Studio on the Boulevard of the Allies. He merged them and relocated both studios to their current locale on Carson Street.

Jenny N. Design, LEATHER, Robin's Nest, 5504 Penn Ave., Pittsburgh 15206; jennyndesign@gmail.com; jennyndesign.com. Jenny Nemlekar came back to making tote bags. (Her mom taught her at age six in her college dorm room while procrastinating from studying.) Ironically, earning a degree in biomedical engineering taught her that she needed to be her own boss. She naïvely thought owning a business would allow her to do what inspired her while creating the flexibility to set her own work schedule. What she didn't realize was that owning a business is a 24/7 commitment and that

industrial sewing machines and leather hides are incredibly heavy. Jenny is an artist by nature and an engineer by discipline, so her business is the fusion of her own artistic aesthetic and the engineering principles gleaned through her education. She designs her bags by sketching the final silhouette in a notebook, then reverse-engineers the design to create a template. Next she cuts the leather and fabric lining and sews and rivets the bag together. She lives and breathes Jenny N. full-time, hand making every single bag one at a time (or in very small batches) in her home studio. Technically, her studio is a 50 x 50-square-foot corner of her (600-square-foot) studio apartment, which she also shares with Shay, her husband, and their large pug, Hubert. She uses premium quality leathers and durable canvases for her bags and totes. Each piece incorporates her classic aesthetic, while minimizing waste and scraps. You can shop Jenny's bags online, or find her creations at various locations and events throughout the country. Check her website for an updated list.

Kid Ewe Knot, KNITTING, 429 Washington Ave., Ste. 4, Bridgeville 15017; (412) 257-2557; kideweknot.com. Open Tues 10 a.m. to 7 p.m.; Wed, 10 a.m. to 2 p.m.; Thurs through Sat 10 a.m. to 5 p.m.; every third Sun, noon to 4 p.m. Heather Metzger is passionate about yarn and knitting. And she'll share her passion with you in an instant. She'll show you a cute baby sweater, then tell you that you, yes you, can make it. If there's a pattern, there's a way is her philosophy. Her knit-loving gang at Kid Ewe Knot sells designer yarns, books, patterns, tools, buttons and closures, finishings, and more. They encourage beginners and experts to celebrate June 13 as National Knit in Public Day. Or if you've never picked up a pair of knitting needles before, on that day they'll teach you for free. They also have classes that teach you how to make hats or socks, dye your yarn, repair mistakes in your knitting, and make a shawl to protect you from the frigid Pittsburgh winters. Her friendly and sage advice has won over local fans who frequented the store when the business used to be called Carol's Needlework.

Kobold USA Watch Company, JEWELRY, 1801 Parkway View Dr., Pittsburgh 15205; (412) 788-2830 or (724) 533-3000; koboldwatch.com. The headquarters are located on 170-acre Merry Oaks Farm and open to the public by appointment; call Mon through Fri between 8:30 a.m. and 4:30 p.m. to arrange a visit. Pennsylvania has a very rich watch history. The Hamilton Watch Company, once based in Lancaster, rivaled Swiss watches in their mechanical quality. Now, Kobold USA Watch Company has located its headquarters in the heart of Amish Pennsylvania. The goal of president Michael Kobold is to bring all operations to Pennsylvania in less than 10 years. Located on the same property as the headquarters is a 3000-square-foot facility that showcases the equipment with which Kobold makes its products.

In 2008, for its 10-year anniversary, Kobold launched a significant contribution to American horology (study of time) with its model called The Spirit of America Automatic. With a majority of the watch manufactured in the United States, this uber-cool timekeeper (just ask *24* hero, Jack Bauer) represents a welcome return to US-made wristwatches. The Spirit of America Automatic is the first Kobold to be designed, engineered, manufactured, and assembled in the US. This watch climbed Mount Everest in support of the Navy SEAL Warrior Fund—a charity that aids families SEALs may leave behind. Kobold also offers a more quirky approach to the very precise art of watchmaking with a timepiece called Pandemonium. The open face of the watch displays its chaos of gears and striations of rhodium filigree. It's a face you'll never get tired of staring at, and it beats looking at your phone for accurate times. The wristband is genuine Louisiana alligator, an out-of-state reptile to be sure. FYI: Pittsburgh had alligators spotted in its Monongahela River in Spring of 2015. They were never found.

Maggie's Farm Rum Distillery, DISTILLERY, 3212A Smallman St., Pittsburgh, 15222; (412) 709-6480; maggiesfarmrum.com. Open Wed through Thurs, 11 a.m. to 7 p.m.; Fri and Sat, 11 a.m. to 10 p.m.; Sun, noon to 4 p.m. Cocktail hours: Fri, 4 to 10 p.m.; Sat, noon to 10 p.m. America's best rum is in Pennsylvania? That's correct and it's right here in Pittsburgh. Formerly Allegheny Distillery, Maggie's is the first commercial rum distillery in the state. And that's dating back to at least Prohibition. You can see the Spanish-made copper pot still that they use for all their products—it's behind their cocktail bar. Tim Russell says that Maggie's Farm rum is meant to be a smooth, yet full-flavored, full-bodied spirit; the use of temperature-controlled fermentation in a 100 percent copper pot still and conservative distillation cuts ensure this. What this means is that when rum is distilled, it's heated, but not too high. The temperature must be maintained or the part of the rum you collect (the fraction) will be bad, as it will contain too much ethanol.

The Original Hot Dog Shop, HOT DOGS, 3901 Forbes Ave., Pittsburgh 15213; (412) 621-7388; theoriginalhotdogshop.com. Open Sun and Mon, 10 a.m. to 9 p.m.; Tues through Sat, 10 a.m. to 1:30 a.m. Sydney and Moe Simon opened their shop in the shadow of the infamous stadium, Forbes Field, when the Pittsburgh Pirates won the 1960 World Series. Additional hot dog stands were eventually opened in Monroeville and Church Falls, Virginia. What makes The Original Hot Dog Stand, or the "O," a great story is the belief that companies are made up of employees who are treated like family. When one of Syd's employees, Nathan Keyes, needed a new liver, he treated the situation as a family emergency. Keyes's shot at a transplant looked pretty grim, and he was given only 18 months to live. But Pennsylvanians can be pretty pushy. Syd petitioned one of the most powerful "CEOs" in the US, President George Herbert Walker Bush. With the president's help, Keyes received a new liver. Syd also dealt with a few of his own health problems, including skin cancer, but he managed to live into his 80s, passing away in 2008. Syd's family continues to work his hot dog stand. But not without fond memories. Syd's daughter, Terry Campasano, said that the "O" is her dad because it was his dream. While hot dogs first made their debut in 1871 on Coney Island, New York, few hot dog stands have lasted as long as the "O" (over half a century). The "O" also serves burgers and french fries and all the typical American fare you'd expect from a family eatery.

Penn Brewery, BREWERY, 800 Vinial St., Pittsburgh 15212; (412) 237-9400; pennbrew.com. Tours by appointment. The restaurant is open Mon through Sat, 11 a.m to midnight; Sun, 11 a.m. to 9 p.m. Penn Brewery considers itself a pioneer in American craft brewing. They began brewing classic lagers and

German beer styles, adhering to the quality standards of the 17th-century Bavarian *Reinheitsgebot* purity laws, which, you may have guessed, are really, really strict. As they've expanded their line of beers to include more contemporary concoctions of chocolate and pumpkin beers, they haven't abandoned their strict attitude. They brew their beers by hand with top-tier barley and hops, which has won them numerous awards throughout the years. Tickets to take a tour of the brewery are available online, but times and space are limited. For $25 you get a tour, a sample, and your choice of T-shirt or growler. You can also visit their restaurant for an "authentic taste of Pittsburgh," but reservations are required.

The Quilt Company, QUILTING, 3940 Middle Rd., Allison Park 15101; (412) 487-9532; thequiltcompany.com. Open Mon, 9:30 a.m. to 9 p.m.; Tues through Sat, 9:30 a.m. to 5 p.m. Karen Montgomery sells quilting supplies, Bernina sewing machines, and Handi Quilter Longarms (large sewing machines that aid in quilting) as well as publishes patterns and books under The Quilt Company name. You can purchase and download the patterns from her website as well. Never wanting any piece to be left behind, Montgomery has patterns called Scrap Crazy, which use leftover fabric from previous projects. Montgomery believes you are never too old or too young to start quilting. She has a Scrap Crazy play book for kids too. Her patterns are deceptively simple looking. But to be a quilter, you must marry precise with colorful whimsy. She does traditional patterns, such as LeMoyne Star (a large star in the center of the quilt), as well as new. One clever pattern that has a contemporary feel to it is a series of beach umbrellas on a shoreline.

Sapling Press, PAPER/STATIONERY, 3524 Butler St., 1st Floor, Pittsburgh 15201; (412) 681-1003; saplingpress.com. Lisa Cairns Krowinski describes herself as "a typography-lovin' graphic designer, turned letterpress-printin' stationery designer who makes the cards for you to give to that one friend of yours who truly gets it." Her tongue-in-cheek attitude flows into her embossed and pressed stationery and occasion cards. But she can be serious and design very classy and hip business cards. Sapling Press is one of the few true print shops that customizes paper products for you and doesn't force you to choose from predesigned templates. It's nice to actually buy (and receive) a card without a Hallmark imprint on the back. As a savvy business person you can show your unique business card, knowing it's not been ordered and generated from a computer website. It's not just about classy logos or witty words, the paper stock that Sapling Press uses is something your fingertips will love to touch—paper with gravitas. They carry different qualities from recycled to linen and smooth to matte finishes. While based in Pittsburgh, Sapling Press has creations in select stores throughout the country. There's a complete list on the website.

Soyil Candles by Greta, CANDLES, 269 Republic St., Pittsburgh 15211; soyilcandles@gmail.com; soyil.com. Candlemaker Greta Falvo openly admits she is obsessed. Eco-friendly (they're all soy) and long-burning, the candles she makes *are* kind of addicting. And that's okay. Their sleek, understated design, in square and round glass holders, looks too commercial to be true, but be assured, they contain no dyes and are all-natural. Greta's scents are seasonal, so they're a lovely way to enjoy Pennsylvania's spring, summer, fall, and winter as you burn your candles. Candle burning began as a way to reduce or mask unwelcomed and unwanted odors in the home and in other enclosed areas. Attention brides (and bridesmaids): Greta offers tiny candles or margarita glass candles as favors for your festive occasions. You can find Greta's creations at different venues throughout the state. Check her website for details.

Studebaker Metals, JEWELRY, 534 Braddock Ave, Braddock 15104; (412) 852-4733; studebakermetals.com. Open Mon through Fri, 10 a.m. to 6 p.m.; Sat, noon to 5 p.m. Studebaker Metals is a traditional metal-smithing workshop. Using classic methods and high-quality materials, they forge and handcraft a collection of unique jewelry that just may make you part with your Alex & Ani. They label their pieces as "utilitarian," but it's more the look of industrial funk. The solid feel of certain cuffs and the cool lightness of their bangles separate them from the mass-produced pieces. Ready for everyday wear, each silver, alloy brass, or alloy copper piece is heated to redefine their shapes. Then the piece comes to life on a pair of antique anvils. The finishes come in brushed mill, a method that brings a hand-brush texture to several of their designs. It creates a distressed work patina or softer striated, almost striped finish. "Work patina" is a piece that is not buffed or polished, but has a natural oxide layer bringing with it unique colors and the look of a distressed piece of metal. It's sort of like the head of a well-used hammer. None of their work is chemically treated. It's all the artisan's hammer and imagination. An heirloom-quality piece forged for you on antique anvils? Not bad for a day's work.

Wigle Whiskey, DISTILLERY, 2401 Smallman St., Pittsburgh 15222; (412) 224-2827; wiglewhiskey.com. The distillery is open Mon through Sat, 10 a.m. to 6 p.m.; Sun, 10 a.m. to 4 p.m. Wigle is a small-batch whiskey distillery that opened in Pittsburgh's Strip District in 2012. This company's logo has a little noose from which the "g" in the word *Wigle* hangs. While the noose may be a bit off-putting, it's there because the owners (whiskey lovers Meredith and Alex Meyer) named the distillery after folk hero Phillip Wigle, who was hung for treason due to his leadership role in the Whiskey Rebellion. Wigle was posthumously pardoned by President George Washington.

The Meyers began distilling in 2011 and opened their family-owned and -operated small business a year later. Wigle was the first distillery to open since the Joseph Finch distillery closed in the 1920s due to pesky Prohibition. According to the general rule of distilling, rye adds spice, wheat adds sweetness, and corn makes the alcohol. The Wigle Distillery crafts ryes, which have to be aged in brand-new charred American Oak barrels. And its bourbon is made with organic Wapsie Valley corn, grown by Weatherbury Farm in Avella. The farm is located in Washington County. Considered frontier in 1760s, it's nestled near the border of West Virginia. If that's not enough reason to sample their spirits, you should know that Wigle is America's most awarded craft whiskey. The American Craft Spirits Association says so.

Armstrong

Insko Leather Shop, LEATHER, 124 Airshaft Rd., Apollo 15613; (724) 845-8072; inskoleather.com. Open Mon through Fri, 3 to 6:30 p.m.; Sat, 10 a.m. to 5 p.m. Transplants to Pennsylvania, Mike and Tammy Insko have always been into leatherwork. Mike is a third generation leather craftsman. From saddle repairs to holsters to belts, the family (including kids Nicholas, Tucker, Jocelyn, and Zachary) is happy to talk hide with anyone. That's why they fit in so well in Pennsylvania. Leather lovers from all over the state (and country) visit and order online from the Insko's selection of items that range in style from the simple and elegant to the ornate and western. If you're not into the look of the leather and prefer a more laid back sort of sport, Insko's son, Zack, ties fishing flies. If you've never felt the tug of a 13-pound brook trout on the end of your fly line—you haven't lived. Pennsylvania is home to some of the best limestone streams on the East Coast. These streams are pure and cold and fast—just the way the trout like them. You may think you're stopping in for a leather belt, but you may come away with fly lures and fish tales.

Beaver

Hoffmans Forge, LLC, BLACKSMITH, 2301 Duss Ave., Ambridge 15003; (724) 251-9320; hoffmansforge.com). James A. (Jymm) Hoffman has a degree in museum studies from Salem College, and has been a blacksmith since 1981. Hoffman specializes in museum quality reproductions and custom orders. Items range from cooking utensils and fireplace equipment to architectural hardware, lighting devices, and tools. He was voted one of the "200 Best Craftsmen" in 1993, '96, '97, and '98 by *Early American Life*. He appears at various craft shows and historical re-enactments demonstrating his art with an authentic reproduction of an 18th-century traveling forge. He also offers hands-on instruction for those interested in learning the blacksmith's trade. Three years in a row, Jymm received a grant to teach an apprentice with the Apprenticeship in Traditional Arts Program from the Pennsylvania Council on the Arts. He also teaches "at risk" kids at Pressly Ridge at Ohiopyle in conjunction with the Pennsylvania Rural Arts Alliance.

McCormack Apiaries, Inc., HONEY, 115 Reesman Dr., Aliquippa 15001; (724) 495-6310; tlmccormack@hotmail.com. Open year-round, but call ahead for availability—you don't want to scare the bees! The McCormacks are one sweet family. They own and operate a honey business, specializing in raw honey, honey products, and beeswax. Most of us think of honey as uniformly gold—but honey is available in many colors and flavors from light gold to red. McCormack's light honey is wildflower, coming from a mixture of spring and early summer blooms. Their dark honey (bamboo red) comes primarily from Japanese knotweed, a plant that grows along the riverbanks and highways of Beaver County. Beekeepers often harvest honey by first "sedating" the bees with small puffs of smoke, which changes a bee's behavior, making them less likely to sting. You probably remember from grade school biology that bees use nectar to make honey. But your recollection of the rest of the process is kind of fuzzy, which might just be a good thing, because the idea of the bees chewing and spitting out the nectar may make you swear off honey forever. Skipping ahead, enter McCormack Apiary, where beekeepers gather the honeycomb frames and scrape off the wax cap that bees use as a plug on top of each cell. Once removed, the frames are placed in an extractor that collects honey from the combs.

McCormack Apiaries sells their honey at the farmers' markets in Ambridge and Beaver in one- to five-pound containers. But that's not all they do. Separate from their business, the McCormack's began a foundation, called the Thomas L. and Linda J. McCormack Foundation. They collect and ship donated medical items to Panama. Tom McCormack spends six months in Panama every year distributing the items and working on fitting prostheses on amputees. To date, they have shipped fifteen 40-foot cargo containers of supplies.

Michael Mootz Candies, CANDY/CHOCOLATE, 1246 Sans Souci Parkway, Hanover Township 18706; (570) 823-8272; michaelmootzcandies.com. Store hours are Mon through Fri, 9 a.m. to 6 p.m.; Sat 10 a.m. to 5 p.m. Extended holiday hours from late Oct to late Dec are Mon through Sat, 9 a.m. to 8 p.m.; Sun 10 a.m. to 5 p.m. Coal's slow, steady burn powered steam engines in the mighty industrial age. As a heat source it's a necessity to keep people and places warm during the bitter winters. Small-scale coal mining began in southwestern Pennsylvania in the mid-1800s. A different kind of "coal" began its rise to fame in the northeastern part of the state. In the 1950s, Pottsville grocers Catherine and George Mootz made too much candy. They took the abundant sweets to their store. The licorice-flavored rock candy, called Black Diamonds, was sold in a little coal bucket with a tiny hammer to "crack" or break up the chunks. Coal candy is a relatively new phenomenon to Pennsylvania, though an oily black confection called G-Shaft Candy had already been sold in Chicago by coal-miner widow turned candymaker, Harriet Williamson, in the 1830s. The Mootz family was so successful in this endeavor that they no longer sell groceries. They've devoted themselves totally to sweets. Their famous candy, now called Anthracite Candy Coal, is a favorite around Christmas, where tradition holds that bad children receive coal in their stockings. For all the good children (and adults) in your life, the shop also makes chocolates and gummy sweet treats year-round.

Bedford

Zimmerman's Country Furniture, FURNITURE, 131 Lingenfelter Rd., Bedford 15522; (814) 623-3303; zimmermanenterprise.com. Open Mon through Fri, 10 a.m. to 7 p.m. What began as a hobby has grown into a lasting legacy. The Zimmermans build authentic country-style furniture. Family-owned and -operated for more than 20 years, the company offers furniture made from wood that is native to Pennsylvania: hickory, oak, pine, cedar, sassafras, and eastern red cedar, and it's all made at their warehouse. "Penn's Woods" wasn't just a quaint name. In the 1700s, about 90 percent of the state was covered with hardwoods, pine, and hemlock trees. Tall and straight, these trees were once in demand for ships masts. Lumbermen made their fortunes as workers seeped through the state to clear-cut the hills. By the 1920s, the trees were almost gone and much of the land was deforested. The Commonwealth bought thousands of acres from the lumber was companies and began to reforest. Today, Pennsylvania's hardwoods are once again in demand, and modern lumbering practices insure the forests will be properly managed. The furniture is reminiscent of your grandpa's cabin interior—sturdy, rustic, and built to last. Don't worry if you fall in love with that rocker and can't strap it to your vehicle—Zimmerman's furniture can be shipped to your home.

Berks

Bill's Khakis, APPAREL, 531 Canal St., Reading 19602; (610) 372-9765; billskhakis.com. Company founder, Bill Thomas, then college student, felt a connection in a pair of original World War II khakis he discovered at an Army surplus store. He loved everything about them—the fit, the pockets, the durability. In the post-college, corporate world, he couldn't find a pair of khakis that measured up. He wanted a pair that not only lasted, but were made in the USA. Clothes that had an American-made quality were hard to come by. Bill was frustrated. In 1990, Bill quit his advertising job, moved from Chicago to Reading, and used savings and the cash from a bunch of part-time jobs (painter, ski lift operator, freelance writer, to name a few) to start Bill's Khakis. He moved into a renovated factory (National Historic Landmark) and now has about 500 employees making not just khakis but all sorts of clothes, jeans, shirts, coats, jackets, vests, and more. The clothes are typically sized for men, as the smallest waist size is 30. But that's not to say women can't find their dream khakis just like Bill. Bill's Khakis are available online and at fine retail stores throughout Pennsylvania, such as Bloomingdale's and Nordstrom.

Butter Valley Harvest, FARMS, 1690 Route 100, Bally 19503; (610) 845-0707; buttervalley harvest.com. **Open Wed, 2 to 4:30 p.m.; Sat, 10 a.m. to noon.** The Ehst Homestead Farm has provided for a variety of consumer needs over the years, growing corn, wheat, lettuce, tomatoes, and oh yeah, butterhead lettuce. It has been home to a dairy operation as well as numerous chickens and pigs. There was a creek-powered mill and a blacksmith shop. It has met the various needs of families who lived here and the surrounding community for generations. Along with his dad, Ryan Ehst has moved the farm into the organic sphere, where they can be stewards of the land they have loved for years. There are three other extended family members who run farming businesses on the historic property. They broke ground on their original three-bay greenhouse in early August 2008 and began growing their first lettuce plants three months later. At the same time, the old red barn that stood to the left of the drive as you came down the lane was torn down to make room for Butter Valley Harvest's packing house and market. Despite the family's sentimental attachment to the structure, the barn, whose beams bore the initials J.E. 1859 and the undated initials H.E., was no longer a stable or safe building. A new pole barn was constructed in November 2008, and houses the beam from the original wooden barn.

Country Additions, FURNITURE, 420 Beacon St., Birdsboro 19508; (610) 404-2062; cacountryfurniture.com. Gallery hours are Mon through Fri, 10 a.m. to 5 p.m.; Sat, 10 a.m. to 4 p.m. Country Additions should probably be renamed Country Addictions, their work is so hard to resist. The have an impressive selection of handmade and custom solid wood furniture, which is all made on site. Vince Suglia and his team of experienced craftsmen have been making pieces for over 20 years using traditional wood-working methods. One of their most charming pieces is called a chimney cabinet. These tall, skinny, shallow cupboards or open cases were originally designed to take advantage of narrow spaces next to fireplaces. The chimney cabinets come with or without doors and can be painted (Country Additions has their own color chart) and distressed or unfinished. Country Additions also makes bedroom suites, kitchen and dining room suites, and custom furniture pieces in primitive and rustic styles. Located along the Schuylkill River in Birdsboro, they are tucked between the rolling hills of southeastern Pennsylvania, about 10 miles outside of Reading.

The Country Seat, Inc., BASKETS, 1013 Old Philly Pike, Kempton 19529; (610) 756-6124; countryseat.com/basketstore.htm. Open Mon, noon to 5 p.m.; Tues, 9 a.m. to 5 p.m.; and select Saturdays, 9 a.m. to 1 p.m. If you're guessing this company makes chairs, you're only half right. The Country Seat is one of the oldest and largest basketry suppliers in the country. Celebrating 40 years in business, it began when Bill Longenecker retired from his "real" job to work with wife Donna on a full-time basis. Their basket supply business grew and Bill took care of things while Donna was away at shows. His most impressive work was a Nantucket basket large enough for daughter Angie to sit inside of. In 1988, the business moved into a new pole building behind the Longeneckers' home. It was large enough to contain store, office, workroom, and warehouse, and although it seemed overly large at the time, it quickly filled with supplies and is now stuffed with all manner of basketry, gourd-weaving, and chair-seating supplies. From wire handles to wooden bases, pine needles to Shaker tape, Irish waxed linen to braided seagrass, you'll find almost everything you need for baskets. You'll also find caned chairs and stools. There's an online catalog of their products so you can browse from the comfort of your home when you can't make it to Kempton.

Eric Claypoole Hexsigns, HEX SIGNS, 227 Schock Rd., Lenhartsville 19534; (610) 562-8911; claypoolehexsigns.com. Visit by appointment only. Barnstars began to appear on barns and farmhouses around the early 1800s with the influx of German "Deutsch" immigrants (dubbed Pennsylvania Dutch). Originally painted as superstitious symbols to protect the farm and/or bring good luck, their true purpose isn't exactly clear. Barnstars are typically found in Berks, Carbon, Lehigh, Montgomery, and Bucks Counties (earliest dated 1819). As the art form was passed down from generation to generation, the interpretations of the symbols changed. When Eric Claypoole took over the family business in 1996, he had already been painting barnstars and hexsigns—one of the last few painters in the country—for about 10 years. Lack of farming and development has destroyed many barns and

the stars with them. A barn star consisted of a star with as few as 4 and as many as 16 points. The 4-point star is supposed to represent the 4 seasons. The 8-point star is associated with marriage and fertility. The 12-point star represents the 12 apostles, and the 16-point star represents prosperity. Elements such as hearts, birds (distle fink), tulips, butterflies, and rosettes were added to represent good luck.

Hexsigns came into existence in the 1940s as a way to make the barnstar a more portable art form. The term hexsign is derived from the Pennsylvania Dutch word hexafoos (witch's foot). Hexsigns are painted on wooden discs (from 8 inches to 4 feet in diameter), contain the same symbols and shapes as barnstars, and can be hung anywhere. No barn for a hexsign? No worries. Eric's 8-inch hexsigns make perfect Christmas ornaments to adorn (and protect) your tree.

Fegley Violin, MUSICAL INSTRUMENTS, 400 W. 37th St., Reading 19606; (610) 779-0665; fegleyviolin.com. Open Mon through Sat, 9 a.m. to 5:30 p.m. With over 35 years serving the stringed instrument community, Fegley's goes above and beyond as an instrument repair shop. Joseph McDevitt handmakes violins, violas, cellos, and their accompanying bows. He also plays them. The unique thing about his instruments is that they are custom built to meet every player's unique personality and preference. Like a good suit, the instrument is made to fit the person; the person is not asked to fit the instrument. Joseph's father, the late James Fegley, founded the store in the 1970s and began offering services such as partial and complete instrument restoration, appraisals of new and old instruments, and even the occasional maintenance instructions—Violin Care 101. Like his father, Joseph believes in holding true to the ways of the old masters. Joseph graduated from the elite North Bennet Street School (NBSS) in Boston as a luthier (NBSS is like the Harvard of career schools). He studied with master craftsmen who knew more about the violin than the musicians who played them. He's not ashamed of the past or tradition, yet he's able to adapt to the new.

GI Bow, BOWS, 19th and Cotton St., Reading 17316; (267) 231-6257; gibow .com. The studio is open year-round; call ahead for hours. War is hell; Justin Steinmetz knows that first hand. In 2008-09 he did his tour of duty as part of Operation Iraqi Freedom. To deal with the drudgery, he obtained a band saw and other pieces of equipment to fashion wooden items. He found his passion in making wood bows and bamboo arrows. Rather than consider the wounded children of Iraqi war as just collateral damage, he reached out to them, showing them how to use his handcrafted bows. He created a sort of Boy and Girl Scouts of Iraq, introducing children to all the adventures of scouting he recalled as a child. Back in the States, he continued making wood bows. At the same time, Brendan Graham was engaged in his own personal war against a groundhog that was killing his dream of becoming a farmer. He fashioned a bow to humanely rid himself of the critter, but enjoyed the process of creating the bow so much that he forgot about the groundhog and found a new dream. He also found Justin (via the Internet) in the hopes he could better his bow-making skills and fill the back orders for his own wood bows. Justin offered Brendan more than advice—he offered him the opportunity to work with him at GI Bow. Brendan grabbed his college roommate Hunter Kessler, and the trio has been successfully making wood bows and arrows since.

Godiva Chocolatier, CANDY/CHOCOLATE, 650 Neversink Rd., Reading 19606; (610) 779-3797; godiva.com. This company has been associated with luxurious and delicious chocolate truffles—and with a naked lady—for more than seven decades. Joseph Draps began his chocolate company in Brussels in the early 1900s. He named his company after the infamous Lady Godiva. She rode naked through the streets (covered only with her hair) to protest the exorbitant taxes that were literally taking the clothes off the backs of the townspeople. It's not clear exactly why Draps used this once publically naked woman to embellish his brand. Maybe because both are luscious and sexy? Most believe it's due to her legendary courage and risk-taking character. In 1966 the Draps family met with the American enterprise, Campbell Soup Company. Seeing (and tasting) the quality chocolate, Campbell's acquired one-third of a stake in Godiva and moved a majority of the production to the US. In 1968, Godiva Chocolatier began large-scale domestic production, using the exclusive Belgian recipes. The company has continued to expand over the years. The Reading plant produces the same amount of chocolate for America as the old Belgian plant produces for everyone else. Godiva is sold in boutiques and online throughout the world. When you visit the Reading shop, be sure to head to the "seconds" section, where you'll find discounted chocolatey mistakes that the company won't sell for full price.

Homespun Woolens, KNITTING, 57 Star Rd., Hereford 19607; (215) 541-0565; facebook.com/homespunwoolens/info. Open Wed through Sat, 10 a.m. to 5 p.m.; Sun, 10 a.m. to 4 p.m. Beware: There are touchy people at Kay Leisey's store. And they are her biggest fans. They love touching her hand-hooked rugs and other hooked designs and creations. They're also touchy about the term "hand-hooked rugs." We're not talking about the latch-hooked rugs that look suspiciously like shag carpets. We're talking Miller or Harman hooks (named after the companies who make them) that almost look like an odd combination of the end of a screwdriver and an ugly knitting needle. And we're talking wool hooked with a simple flick of the wrist, in and out of a fabric base of monk's cloth or linen. These hand-hooked pieces from Kay's store are supple and warm—they can go on the floor, on a wall, or on top of your table. They are also sturdy. Kay is sure they'll last longer than anything machine made. She believes in creating heirlooms. And she does so happily in her 1800s barn. You can meet "touchy" people anywhere—artisans and appreciators who love the quality and texture of a hand-hooked rug. Yet, there's no need for Kay or her Homespun Woolens store to leave Pennsylvania. Her hooking roots are here, her family is here, and there's plenty of wool to keep her busy.

Jonathan's Wooden Spoons, WOODWORKING, 3716 Route 737, Kempton 19529; (800) 776-6853; woodspoon.com. From Bryn Athyn, Pennsylvania, to Bath, Maine, then back to Pennsylvania, Jonathan Simons has always had his hands on wood. Because it is so cold in Maine, Simons was forced to design single piece works because he couldn't successfully glue the legs of the stools he was making (the glue doesn't work in cold temperatures). He moved south to Pennsylvania and for 35 years he's been designing, creating, and testing wooden spoons. His spoons are primarily made of cherry wood—a wood that's plentiful and good to work with. Long ago, as farmers clear-cut huge swaths of land to plant their fields, wild cherry trees grew up along the fence and tree lines. Pennsylvania is now queen of cherry wood. And *cherry* is a great word, Simons adds, reminding him of the word "cheerful." Cherry is a hard wood with a handsome color, close-grained, durable, and strong. Since Simons cooks, he understands the need for a well-balanced

utensil; one with a good feel and clean edge. His utensils are unique because they are designed with the human hand and specific purpose in mind. With an eye toward innovation, he makes some spoons that latch on to the side of a pot or pan. Simons also dabbles in the whimsical, creating spoons with wiggly, striped "cat tail" handles. His line of spoons has expanded to include salad forks and spoons, tongs, spatulas, spaghetti forks, spreaders, and more. He admits you can easily buy cheaper, machine-made spoons. And sure, they'll work. But for Simons, the best utensils to have in your home are the ones that have the imprint of the human spirit. When a real person takes the time and care to craft a one-of-a-kind piece, you have a something with "soul." You can purchase Jonathan's Wooden Spoons online, at craft shows, and in stores throughout the country, including many in Pennsylvania. Visit his website for a complete list.

Robesonia Redware, CERAMICS/POTTERY, 40 West Penn Ave., Robesonia 19551; (610) 693-8084; robesoniaredware.com. Open Thurs through Sat, 10 a.m. to 6 p.m.; Sun through Wed by appointment only. It's good to be able to play with "dirt" on a daily basis. Potters Scott Madeira and his sons Thilo Schmitz and Curt Pearson do just that, producing top-of-the-line Pennsylvania German Redware from traditional reproductions and their own designs. The trio has created pieces ranging from handmade figurines to *sliptrailed* (like drippings) and *sgraffitoed* (scuffed or scratched) plates, vessels, and slab-built works of art. Scott has been honored to have his redware ornaments selected to hang on the White House Christmas tree. Redware captured the imagination of Thilo and Curt, who have been throwing all sorts of pottery. Check their website for a list of events across the area where you'll find their treasures. Of course be sure to visit their showroom, where they also feature other local artists such as Furnace Creek Forge, Handwerk Tin, Bennett Street Baskets, 1860 Wood Company, Madeira Oil Paintings, Robesonia Wicks, and many more.

Tom Sturgis Pretzels, PRETZELS, 2267 Lancaster Pike, Reading 19607; (610) 775-0335; tomsturgispretzels.com. Store hours are Mon through Sat, 8:30

a.m. to 5:30 p.m. Parties of 10 or more must call first to arrange a tour. The first American commercial pretzel bakery was founded by Julius Sturgis in Lititz, Pennsylvania in 1861, where he developed a crispy (hard) pretzel recipe. Although Julius passed away in 1897, his descendants continue the pretzel-baking tradition. In 1946, grandson Marriott "Tom" Sturgis, founded the Tom Sturgis Pretzel Company after years of learning pretzel baking from his family members. His son (also called Tom) joined the company. Now five generations of pretzel baking has earned the Sturgis family the nickname of "First Family of Pretzels." Pretzels were originally made by hand from start to finish. As technology progressed, parts of the procedure were mechanized. Through all these changes (from hand twisting at a top speed of 40 pretzels per minute to thousands of pretzels per minute) pretzels remain a favorite, healthy snack food. Marriott "Tom" Sturgis was responsible for bringing the Sturgis pretzel baking family to Reading in the 1920s. Under new management, this historic bakery (built in 1784) offers visitors a glimpse of what it was like for Julius Sturgis to bake pretzels in the "old days." Listed on the National Register of Historic Places, it provides interactive demonstrations, reproduction equipment, and historical photographs. You'll learn everything you ever wanted to know about pretzels—and more.

Blair

Benzel's Pretzel Bakery, PRETZELS, 5200 Sixth Ave., Altoona 16602; (814) 942-5062; benzels.com. Factory Outlet Store open Tues through Fri, 9 a.m. to 5 p.m.; Sat, 10 a.m. to 1 p.m. For over 100 years this pretzel bakery has been making, well, pretzels. Hard pretzels to be specific. The Benzel family is well known for their Pennysticks—hard pretzels that aren't knotted but straight—to twirl in mustard or the condiment of your choice. The hard pretzel begins its life as sourdough and then is baked much like a soft pretzel. But toward the end of the process, the hard pretzels are baked longer, essentially drying out the dough to achieve that crunchiness that keeps your molars happily munching. Young German immigrant Adolph Benzel founded the Benzel Bakery in 1911. While he made other foods besides pretzels, the hard pretzels were the local favorite. The company still uses his recipe, although technology has been incorporated to keep up with increased demand. The company makes over 50 million pretzels daily. They've introduced products such as saltless pretzels, soy pretzels, oat bran pretzels, and honey wheat pretzels. Pretzels are the second most popular snack in the world. They're also low in fat and calories.

Boyer Candy Company, CANDY/CHOCOLATE, 821 17th St., Altoona 16602; (814) 944-9401; boyercandies.com. Open Mon through Sat, 10 a.m. to 6 p.m.; Sat, 11 a.m. to 4 p.m. The company that invented Mallo Cups (and those addicting coin cards) is nestled in the hills of central Pennsylvania. It was started by two brothers, Bill and Bob, who grew up creating tasty fudge and nut clusters and many other different types of candy and decided to turn it into a lucrative business. But the one thing that had the brothers stumped was marshmallow. They couldn't get the darn stuff to cooperate and stay still. Their very wise mother, Emily, told them to use cupcake holders to keep things in place, and bingo! The first "cup" candy (even before Reese's Peanut Butter Cup), Mallo Cup, was born. So popular was the candy that the brothers moved their operation to a factory in the mid-1930s. They also introduced the Play Money program. Money was still tight in postwar America, so the Boyers decided to give kids free candy. The cardboard that supported the candy cups was stamped with a coin value, from a nickel to a dollar. In exchange for saving up their "money," kids could redeem the cardboard coins for candy. This program, similar to the Green Stamps, is still in effect today, but now you can get more than free candy. Sweatshirts, watches, hats, and tote bags are all traded for Mallo Cup coins.

Bradford

Beckwith Maples, MAPLE, 862 Captain Moore Rd., Rome 18837; (570) 247-7475; maple-syrup.com. **Hours are seasonal; call before visiting.** Phillip Beckwith wants you to try his Maple Crumb Sugar in place of brown sugar. He's certain it will add a special touch to your baked goods, sides, and main dishes. And he'd like you to be generous with his Maple Cream, which makes a delicious spread for toast and muffins.

At Beckwith Maples, things get crazy during spring. There are two different wood lots with 2,400 taps dripping sap, which is run through pipelines to stainless steel tanks. Maple syrup is not just for breakfast any more. It's a traditional sweetener rich in nutrients, and it's a much better choice than most of the cheap, highly processed pancake toppers currently on supermarket shelves—most are just caramel-colored corn syrup. Grade B maple syrup is darker and more nutrient-dense than Grade A, and is preferred for its nutritional value. Similar to any other plant-based product, look for maple syrup produced in small batches by small-scale producers who follow sustainable and organic practices, where the maple trees are part of a natural diversified forest.

Pennsylvania Quilter, QUILTING, 375 N. Center St., Canton 17724; (570) 244-8097; northwind00@hotmail.com; bettyneff.com. It's a couple that was meant to be. Betty and Richard Neff have been threaded together for years. Betty quilts as well as designs and sells her own line of quilting patterns. She has lectured and taught quilting workshops and retreats. She's written many quilt magazine articles and her book of vintage quilting patterns, *Quilts to Treasure,* is available on Amazon. She works with museums to increase public knowledge of the art of quilting. Richard keeps her running—he restores and sells vintage sewing machines. Singer Featherweights are his specialty. For the couple quilting is more than a business, it's a passion. They restore vintage quilts and do what they can to make sure that this textile art is appreciated and continued. Quilts, which have three basic parts—patchwork top, filler or batting, and the bottom or backing—weren't simply blankets. While a quilt kept the body warm, it evolved into a fabric art with function. Some quilts served as decorative wall hangings. The very activity of quilting brings people together, as it requires creative thinking and problem solving. Patterns became intricate, symbolic, and unique. A finished quilt was handed down from one generation to the next. A quilt given to a couple as a wedding gift became an instant heirloom. Betty and Richard keep the love and process of quilting alive while preserving its history.

Bucks

Alfa & Omega Winery, WINERY, 3612 Stump Rd., Doylestown 18902; (215) 249-1438; alfaomegawinery.com; Tastings are Fri and Sat, 2 to 7 p.m.; Sun, noon to 4 p.m. Rich Adamek and his family opened their winery in 2012, and it's as unique as his personal history. Adamek grew up in Slovakia, a mountainous country sandwiched between Poland and Hungary that split from Czechoslovakia in 1993. There, he learned the wine trade as a teenager and brought the Eastern European tradition of wine-making to the rolling hills of Southeastern Pennsylvania. There's a pretty little picnic spot on the property where you can enjoy the view as well as the wine. Rich offers the familiar Rieslings and Pinots and the very rare Lemberger wine (often designated as Blauer Limberger). It's a hearty grape that's typically grown in the Danube Valley of southeastern Germany. It produces a wine deep red in color but surprisingly dry and floral. Rich's Lemberger is also spicy and smoky. Like a new breed, the wine world has not yet decided on exactly what a true Lemberger should look or taste like. But you can make up your own mind when you stop in for a sip. Call ahead though, to make sure it's available. Rich makes small batches, he's not a big fan of mass production.

Asher's Chocolates, CANDY/CHOCOLATE, 80 Wambold Rd., Souderton 18964; (215) 721-3000; ashers.com. Chocolate-making is an arduous undertaking. The work is never ending; probably because the by-product is consumed so quickly. Luckily, Asher's Chocolates has been making fine chocolates and candy confections since 1892. The company has proudly earned the title of the oldest family-owned and -operated candy manufacturer in the US. There's something to that. Many candymakers have changed hands, or were unable to survive economic hardships, The Great Depression, two world wars, and other disasters that put them out of business forever. Asher's managed to prosper in spite of the all the difficulties. Today, you can watch chocolate treats being made right before your eyes. Free self-guided multimedia tours of Asher's new state-of-the-art facility are available to the public, just call ahead if you have a group larger than ten. If you're not near Souderton, there's another shop in Lewistown. Formerly known as Goss Candies, this store has all the Asher's Chocolates favorites and more.

Byers' Choice, FIGURINES, 4355 County Line Rd., Chalfont 18914; (215) 822-6700; byers choice.com. **Museum and store hours are Mon through Sat, 10 a.m. to 5 p.m.** All sorts of fun and festive handmade figurines are designed and made on site at Byers' Choice—something for every occasion, season, and holiday. But nothing says Christmas more than Byers' most popular figurines, the "Carolers." These one-foot-high, clay and fabric dolls are inspired by characters from Charles Dickens's *A Christmas Carol.* You'll be able to purchase the memorable Jacob Marley, Tiny Tim, The Ghost of

Christmas Future, and, of course, Ebenezer Scrooge (your choice of the grumpy or happy Scrooge or both). You even have the option of "designing" your own Caroler. They aren't kidding about the "choice" thing.

Clutter started the Byers' business. Joyce Byer loved Christmas, so much so that she'd make a cluster of decorative holiday-inspired dolls from bits of clay and scraps of cloth. The dolls would take up most of the dining room table, spread to the floor, then nearby furniture. Joyce began giving them away as gifts. Soon the dolls became so endearing and desirable, she began to sell them. The decorative delight in Christmas became a full-time business. The figurines now include quaint items such as angels, cats, popcorn machines, and sandcastles. Many are decked out in 1800s period clothes, others look more contemporary such as one couple called "Auntie Esther" and "Auntie Esther's Beach Boyfriend."

Ely Farm, FARMS/DAIRY, 401 Woodhill Rd., Newtown 18940; (215) 860-0669; elyporkproducts.com. Open Thurs and Fri, 9 a.m. to 5 p.m.; Sat, 9 a.m. to 2 p.m. They might tempt you with pork at Ely Farm, but their cheeses cannot be ignored. Their selection includes Aldan's Blessing, a soft and creamy Trappist-style cheese, made in the same way as the monasteries made cheese wheels for hundreds of years. There's Makefield, a savory and lightly sweet soft cheese made in much the same way as Gruyere and aged over 8 months. Washington's Crossing Cheese is a sweet, creamy cheese that hints at Parmigiano and is named in honor of General George Washington's daring surprise attack on the Hessians in New Jersey. He crossed the Delaware River under the cover of darkness, marched to Trenton, and attacked the Hessian outposts in and around Trenton. By 6 p.m., 2,400 troops had begun crossing the ice-choked river. The operation was slow and difficult. There was an abrupt change in the weather forcing the men to fight their way through sleet and a blinding snowstorm. Against all odds, Washington and his men successfully completed the crossing and marched into Trenton on the morning of December 26, achieving a resounding victory over the Hessians. By moving ahead with his bold and daring plan, Washington reignited the cause of freedom and gave new life to the American Revolution.

Farm Furniture, FURNITURE, 1880 South Easton Rd., Doylestown 18901; (570) 854-2102; pafarmfurniture.com. **Hours are Thurs through Sat, 10 a.m. to 5 p.m.; Sun, noon to 5 p.m.** In a converted one-room school house that was built in 1879, Robert Burmeister set up his warehouse. He shares part of it with a women's boutique called Crystal Cottage. And suits him just fine. One furniture survey showed that over 75 percent of respondents who selected furnishings for the home were women.

Robert has over 20 years experience in creating indoor home furnishings in the tradition of Shaker design. Each piece is hand fitted. And hold on to your hats, he's now adding softer tones to his pieces for the shabby chic lovers. Robert's styles do take an interesting journey from Shaker to Colonial and from primitive to eclectic. He's even got pieces that combine one or two styles. He encourages mixing and matching to suit your personal style. His collection of wooden kitchen islands will make you want to remodel your kitchen. Luckily, he does cabinet designs as well. The emphasis on his furniture is beautiful and functional. Robert has made it all—night tables, coffee tables, kitchen tables, chairs, hutches, shelves, chests, entertainment centers, and more. Visit his showroom to see for yourself.

Giggling Goat Dairy, DAIRY, 693 Bucks Rd., Perkasie 18944; (215) 249-4838; gigglinggoatdairy.com. Visiting hours by appointment only. Happy goats make delicious cheese. Or rather the happy people who surround them make the cheese. The goats pretty much graze, and yes, giggle. However, Teri Jones is serious about her respect for nature. Her do-no-harm philosophy includes the land, the animals, their neighbors, and you. They don't use pesticides or herbicides on their fields, barn, or home. She employs rotational grazing as a technique to keep the

herd healthy. The herds are moved from field to field; kind neighbors open their land in order to keep the pastures healthy and growing. Making goat cheese is a very basic task. You milk the goats, bring the milk to room temperature, add some culture (i.e., *lactococcus* bacteria) and a couple of drops of rennet (an enzyme), give it a quick stir, cover the pot, and set it aside for about a day. You drain the mixture through a cheesecloth-lined strainer, salt it, and serve. Simple, right? Just do that about every day on each of the 20 or so goats and you've got enough to make it a commercial business. Then there's the milk testing that has to be done monthly and traveling to farmers' markets to sell the cheese. Not so simple, but it makes Teri (and her customers) happy to be a part of sustainable agriculture.

Jaye's Barkery, PETS, 264 South County Line Rd., Souderton, 18964; (267) 342-2452; jayesbarkery.com. Open Tues through Sat, 10 a.m. to 7 p.m. Jaye Fissel opened her doors in 2009, to both two- and four-legged customers. She makes doggie treats with the promise that nothing artificial is included in any of her products. Each treat is hand-rolled and cut. Like people, dogs are vulnerable to diseases like cancer, diabetes, and kidney and heart disease. Diet plays a huge role in the prevention of these diseases. Jaye assures her customers that her treats contain healthy antioxidants to combat most doggie diseases. Veterinarians also insist that their patients eat healthy and exercise. No table scraps or processed snacks are allowed. Enter Jaye's Bakery, where you can buy healthy treats without the worry of negatively affecting your dog's health. Honestly, the last person you want to see suffer is that little heart-stealer, who has made indelible paw prints on your heart.

Knitting to Know Ewe, KNITTING, 2324 Second Street Pike, Penns Park 18943; (215) 598-9276; knittingtoknowewe.com. Open Tues through Fri, 11 a.m. to 6 p.m.; Sat, 10 a.m. to 5 p.m.; and Sun, 11 a.m. to 4 p.m. Their store is located in the heart of Bucks County, one of the oldest settled parts of the state. Sir William Keith's (second governor of Pennsylvania) estate is still maintained here. It's no coincidence that a yarn store would spring up here either—plenty of rolling hills, farms, and sheep for woolen yarn. The building in which the store is was built in the 1830s and was the town hall of Penns Park, then the post office and general store. It has a warm, inviting atmosphere, and is filled to the brim with beautiful yarns. The staff are always delighted to help out any knitters or crocheters who walk through the door. They've got experience, tools, and skeins of yarn. They can help you with anything from the purchasing of materials to the instruction of a tough project. Although they'd love it if you buy their yarn and supplies, they will help you even if you've purchased your yarn elsewhere.

oWowCow Creamery, DAIRY, 4105 Durham Rd., Ottsville 18942; (610) 847-7070; owowcow.com. Open daily, 11 a.m. to 10 p.m. This creamery makes organic ice cream by hand. It was quite the change of careers for founder and owner John Fezzuolgio, who started out as a graphic designer in Manhattan. He envisioned an ice cream shop that supported the farms and cows that would surround it. Something that offered an organic and healthy option along with a "wow" factor. They now have stores in Ottsville, Wrightstown, and across the Delaware River in Lambertville, New Jersey. Practically a franchise, oWowCow has developed quite a following. Shira Tizer is the general manager of the creamery in Ottsville, and she's definitely not lactose intolerant. A fan of ice cream, Shira is also a fan of the community that enjoys the creamery's product. She and the staff have smiles on their faces even before the customers walk in.

Making real, premium ice cream requires separating the cream (fat) from the milk. You may be surprised to see fresh milk—it looks a bit yellowish versus the pure white we're used to seeing in our store-bought containers. The cream naturally rises up in milk because it's pure fat and lighter than the rest of the components of milk. The cream is easily skimmed from the top and cooled. Ingredients such as sugar, salt, and vanilla are added, then things can get a little interesting. oWowCow has 24 standard flavors in their cases at all times, but can have up to 40 flavors depending on the season.

William Henry Ornamental Ironworks, IRONWORKS, 524 Davisville Rd., Willow Grove 19090; (215) 659-1887; ironworksonline.com. **Open Mon through Fri, 8 a.m. to 4:30 p.m.; Sat and Sun by appointment.** Bill uses a true iron forge to create ornamental gates, railings, indoor and outdoor pieces, and furniture for commercial and residential properties. He's produced whimsical and ornate designs for house and garden. There's a machine shop on-site that can finish or repair your home's new or old ironwork. He's restored and added to the iron works in buildings in the city, such as the Philadelphia Cricket Club and the Baldwin School (an all-girls school founded in 1888). His metalwork is appreciated by iron fans across the nation. In 2002, The History Channel profiled them in the *Hands-On History* program, an episode that followed the history and evolution of various trades in America, most specifically ironworks. They started with the "heat-and-beat" blacksmithing to state-of-the-art machine fabrication of steel products. As a fourth-generation iron shop, they understand history and the evolution of metalwork and technology. Henry's great-grandfather founded the business in Philadelphia during the Great Depression. The facility moved to Willow Grove in the 1960s. William Henry Ornamental Ironworks offers free estimates, planning, and design to match your decor, whether it's Old World Style ornate or modern and sleek.

Butler

Frankferd Farms Foods, FARMS, 717 Saxonburg Blvd., Saxonburg 16056; (724) 352-9510; frankferd.com. **Open Mon through Fri, 9 a.m. to 5:30 p.m.** In 1954 Murray Ferderher had to make an emergency landing on a huge tract of land in western Pennsylvania. He looked around, loved it, and bought the land and the farm and called it Frankferd Farms. He and his wife left their professions (doctor and pharmacist) and became tillers of the land. In 1976, when his son T. Lyle found out that his dad was selling off pieces of the farm to pay for his college education, he and wife Betty dropped out of college and moved back home to help preserve what was left. Three years later when T. Lyle's son Jeremy was born, they took things in a different direction and started Frankferd Farms Milling to enter the budding organic market milling healthy grains. In the process, Frankferd Farms Foods warehouse was launched. Their business grew steadily and they now offer everything from baby food to sauerkraut. They sell to markets, wholesalers, and you. In June, they installed a 10-kilowatt solar array onto the roof of the barn. The solar panels power the home, farm, and flour mill, making Frankferd Farms healthy, organic, and green.

Harmony Grove Farm, FARMS, 175 Harmony Grove Ln., Harrisville 16038; (814) 385-6492; hgfarm.com. Open Mon through Fri, 9 a.m. to 3 p.m. Hours are seasonal though, so be sure to call ahead. Monty and Akemi Hoffman love their farm jokes and puns. Their tagline "Lettuce Eat Natural," is their wink and a nudge reminder that consuming foods (like lettuce) high in vitamins E and B and minerals like potassium is the best way to maintain good health. But growing good greens is a serious business. Organic farms have to jump through a lot of hoops in order to be certified. Monty's great-great grandfather started this farm in the late 19th century. And while the Hoffmans love the old ways of cultivating the soil, they aren't afraid to embrace technology. In their new greenhouse, they produce 800 heads of lettuce per week. That's due to the all-natural hydroponic system—a gentle watering system that allows the produce to float and grow directly in water. So even in summer when the fields are dry, their greenhouse produce is adequately hydrated. While you're there, take a peek at the purple wood products, under the name Hoffman's Wooden Wood. A self-taught woodworker, Akemi was born in Japan and came to the US in the summer of 1998. She was always interested in the world of art and loved creating since she was a kid. She has won prizes for her artwork, including wooden art pieces. She decided to take her career path as a woodworker after experiencing several different careers. Her design is contemporary but has a hint of her traditional cultural background. She sticks to Pennsylvania hardwoods, such as cherry, maple, walnut, and oak to maintain the best quality and also to bring out the highest beauty of the grain. Her purple collection includes mirrors, jewelry boxes, and wooden items that are stained a bold, rich purple. You can check out some of her work online at woodenwood.com or contact her at info@woodenwood.com.

The Metal Peddler, METALWORKS, 110 Miller School Ln., West Sunbury 16061; (866) 500-9898; themetalpeddler.com. Studio hours by appointment only. The Metal Peddler is a small family-owned and -operated company that provides quality handcrafted copper work. Jason Fannin is a master craftsman who started working with metal as a machinist and fabricator. Deciding to set up his own shop, Fannin spent many years learning to work with metal using hand tools, machines, and the simple properties of metal to manipulate it into a particular shape. He's made functional pieces such as copper fence caps, but he has also produced metal fountains and outdoor lanterns. He admits it's not something you can learn by reading a book or just by watching. You have to get into the work by being hands-on, which sometimes means failure. Skill, integrity, and craftsmanship aren't words he uses lightly. The Industrial Age put many craftsmen and apprentices out of work. Jason does his best to stick to their methods and work ethic. He sells his handmade items to folks around the world. The response he has gotten has been outstanding to say the least. More than anything though, he's happy that his work is in people's homes, especially their kitchens. He fabricates custom copper range hoods and backsplashes as well as garden items. Whenever possible, he combines old materials found at the scrap yard or renovation sites with new materials to create his masterpieces.

Woof Stop Barkery, PETS, 139 Hunter Dr., Cranberry Township 16066; (412) 600-2148; woofstop.com. Open year-round, call ahead for orders and pick-ups. Woof Stop Barkery, located north of Pittsburgh, is a great place to make a pit stop for your pet. Nancy Hans started making doggie treats in 2001 when she shared her recipes with her dogs (a.k.a., the Barkery Taste Testers) during the holiday season. She felt the need to do something "special" for her best friends since they brought so much fun and joy into her home and life. So, to the kitchen she went to bake them some tasty treats, and she never stopped. The treats kept coming—and going. Nancy's homemade dog treats are baked right in her home kitchen. When she says, "from my home to yours," she means it. Since her first batch of treats in 2001, Nancy has been researching healthy, quality ingredients that dogs would enjoy and those that are good for them, too. After many positive woofs, wags, and wiggles, Nancy decided it was time to offer her treats to dogs everywhere. Visit her website to order and Nancy will ship her treats to your door, any time of the year.

Cambria

Denny Edwards Wood Turnings, WOODWORKING, Johnstown, 16002; denny@dennyedwards.com; dennyedwards.com. About 45 years ago Denny Edwards was searching for a nice wooden chess set. Unable to find one, he bought a wood lathe and made his own. He figured if he turned enough pawns, eventually he'd get eight that matched. He became very good at woodworking and was inspired by a Dale Nish book on segmented turning. It inspired him to try some new techniques, and he was hooked. But he went overboard and bought exotic lumber from all over the world. Unfortunately, he had a severe reaction to cocobolo wood and ended up in the hospital. He couldn't get near the lathe or saw dust. So his wife cleaned up the sawdust and shavings, covered the lathe, and it sat unused for about 40 years. Upon retirement, Denny decided to give segmented wood turning another try. He used smaller pieces and local wood. But that wasn't enough for him. He decided to dabble in another medium, and nagging from some of his friends pushed him into videotaping. It was tough for Denny to put into words what he was doing, so he taped his work sessions and sent the videos to them. The friends then suggested, since he already had a website, to load the videos there—for everyone. And then to a YouTube channel. Heads-up, though, Dennis Edwards is also the name of the lead singer with the Temptations, so watch your search. You won't see anything about segmented wood bowls—but you'll hear some awesome music if you click on the wrong one! Denny Edwards is happy to say that unlike his namesake, he doesn't take requests, but creates segmented wood pieces that make him happy.

Carbon

Bradford Clocks, Ltd, JEWELRY, **1080 Hudson Dr., Weatherly 18255; (570) 427-4493; bradfordclocks.com. Open Mon through Fri, 9 a.m. to 5:00 p.m.** Leo Humenick, Sr. dedicated himself to fine woodworking. In 1970, when that interest was distilled into a single passion—making the finest quality wood clock cabinets in the US—Leo started his own business. His sons, Dan and Leo, Jr., also became committed to the challenge of creating exquisite clock cabinets that would stand the test of time (pun intended). The trio of talented woodworkers work side by side at Bradford Clocks. They are united in a simple, old-fashioned desire to be the best. This vision is shared by all of Bradford Clocks' employees. From design and assembly to rough cut and sanding, to staining and polishing, the men and women at Bradford Clocks are dedicated to excellence in fine clocks. Traditional-style clocks with a modern appeal, Bradford clocks embody traditional American values of quality craftsmanship, performance, and durability that are part of our country's heritage. While many of Bradford's clocks and timepieces are classic traditional-style clocks, some may be considered antique-style clocks or antique reproduction clocks. Bradford draws inspiration from the classic-style clocks that have become sought after throughout time, and uses that inspiration to design every Bradford clock.

Wild Creek Bee Farm, HONEY, **845 Station St., Lehighton 18235; (570) 527-0863; wildcreekbeefarm.com. Open Mon through Thurs, 6 a.m. to 7 p.m.; Fri,**

6 a.m. to 8:30 p.m.; Sat, 9 to noon. Leave a kid loose with a Mason jar and you never know what will happen. Chris Maxwell used to chase and catch bees (ouch) collecting them in his jars. These days, he's no longer chasing and confining them to jars. On friendlier terms with bees, he collects only honey in jars. Studies have shown that in order to reduce your allergies (severity and incidence) you should consume local honey. It makes sense. If you are allergic to local pollen, your immune system will recognize the familiar pollen that's in the local honey. Another good thing about Wild Creek Bee Farm, like other honey shops in Pennsylvania, is that they pack their own honey. This means there's a hands-on quality control that may be missing at large packing and processing plants. You can order Wild Creek Honey online or ask Chris questions via email. Don't expect a quick response; his honey bees take up a lot of his attention—especially since they chase him now.

Centre

Berkey Creamery at Penn State, DAIRY, Pennsylvania State University, College of Agricultural Sciences, University Park 16801; (814) 8654700; creamery .psu.edu. Open Mon through Thurs, 7 a.m. to 10 p.m.; Fri, 7 a.m. to 11 p.m.; Sat, 8 a.m. to 11 p.m., Sun, 9 a.m. to 10 p.m. In a land where Holstein dairy cows reign supreme, it's not surprising that the state's leading educational institution should produce arguably one of the best ice creams. Each year, 4.5 million pounds of milk (just under a million gallons) flow through the dairy processing facility located on campus. The creamery also makes cheese—which pairs well with any one of the wines from over 170 wineries in the state. Penn State is serious about dairy and has performed decades of research into the processing and pasteurization of milk products. They offer 100 flavors. That many choices may be overwhelming, as plain old vanilla is their most popular seller. Note: if you're a Penn State alum, you are required to try the Alumni Swirl (vanilla ice cream with Swiss mocha chips and blueberry swirled throughout). If you're not planning a visit to cheer on the Nittany Lions, you can always buy their ice cream by the half-gallon online.

Chester

Amazing Acres Goat Dairy, DAIRY, 184 Grove Rd., Elverson 19520; (610) 913-7002; amazingacresgoatdairy.com. Farm visits by appointment only. Will and Lynne Reid run this farm that creates fresh and aged artisan goat cheeses inspired by classic French styles. Amazing Acres' goats are fed on pasture, grain, and hay. They get plenty of daily exercise, fresh air, love, brushings, and treats. Will and Lynne allow the kids to remain with their mothers for at least three months. This means that they lose a bit of milk, but they're okay with that. They understand that this practice produces healthier kids and happier mothers and reduces stress (and separation anxiety) on both. Yes, animals do feel stress and it's evident when goats and kids are separated too early and then the moms produce less milk. Their goats receive no hormones, steroids, antibiotics, or any drugs unless medically necessary. They consider their "girls and boys" to be part of the staff and family. Will and Lynne sell their cheese through the Amazing Acres website, at farmers' markets, and in several local stores. Check their website for a complete list. They welcome visitors to their farm, but request that you either call or email first to arrange a visit.

Herr Foods, Inc., POTATO CHIPS, 20 Herr Dr., Nottingham 19362; (610) 932-9330; herrs.com Open Mon through Thurs, 9 a.m. to 3 p.m.; Fri, 9 to 11 a.m. Hours are subject to change, however, so be sure to call first. Twenty-one-year-old James Stauffer Herr bought a small potato chip company in Lancaster County in 1946 for $1,750. He primarily made chips and pretzel snacks, but his operation grew steadily larger. In 1964 Herr went big. He started to sell the chips in 20-ounce, cardboard "barrels." He offered 2 cellophane bags of chips in one box for 49 cents.

In 1968, the company added 23,000 square feet to its plant, and another 8,000 square feet to the stockrooms. While the gas shortage in the 1970s forced the company to reduce routes and discontinue the barrel (it wasn't a cost effective design when it came to delivery mileage), they rebounded with new products. Snacks such as pretzels, corn chips, cheese curls, and tortilla chips were added to the company's line. And they introduced a clever "waste disposal" system—Herr partnered with farmers who used his potato peels mixed with grain as feed for their steer. Today Jim's son James is the company CEO. Plan a trip to their visitor center to get a tour of the factory.

J. Maki Winery, WINERY, 200 Grove Rd., Elverson 19520; (610) 286-7754; jmakiwinery.com. Open Mon through Sat, 10 a.m. to 5 p.m.; Sun, 12:30 to 5 p.m. It began with a gift and ended with Champagne. In 1973, Janet Maki accepted a wine press from an elderly neighbor when family members showed no interest. Add a small shipment of Zinfandel grapes from California to her basement in Philadelphia, and the experiment began.

A childhood summer on her maternal grandmother's Ohio farm created an enchantment for plant life, and an interest in the natural sciences was cultivated in college. Laboratory skills were developed working at the University of Pennsylvania in medical research, her first career path. The opportunity for experimentation presented itself in a college classmate, who had begun a vineyard in the Finger Lakes region of New York with the planting of white French-American hybrid vines. Each harvest, Janet would help in the picking and pressing, and would bring the juice home for winemaking experiments, all the while gathering vineyard knowledge. Almost 20 years of knowledge and experience (still as a hobby) later, she began to search for land for a vineyard. The Brandywine Valley, with its well-drained schist soil and a low clay component provided the proper bed structure, and a 13-acre parcel was available with a lofty, south-facing slope on which wine grapes thrive. In 1991, with one row of chardonnay, one acre of pinot noir, and one-half acre of vidal blanc planted, the J. Maki Winery at French Creek Ridge Vineyard was born. Twenty-seven months later the first Champagne was offered for sale. In 2001 Janet

Maki became the first, and only, American winemaker ever to be honored with the gold medal for Champagne at the Olympics of wine competition, the Vinales Internationales in Paris, France.

September Farm Cheese, DAIRY, 5287 Horseshoe Pike, Honey Brook, 19344; (610) 273-3552; septemberfarmcheese.com. Open Mon through Sat, 7 a.m. to 8 p.m.; Sat, 7 a.m. to 5 p.m. Dave Rotelle decided to try his hand at making cheese for the first time. This idea wasn't just a Saturday afternoon activity; this man in the kitchen was a man on a mission. This had been the culmination of a dream spurred after visiting cheesemakers in New England while on a family trip. With a basic cheese making kit and recipe in hand, Dave produced the first small wheel of cheese in his farmhouse kitchen. The next step was to pursue a family business so his children could one day call it their own. It was part of a desire to carry on the Rotelle family name that had served the food industry for what became the fourth generation. Dave's mother, Joy, enjoyed offering private catering and cooking lessons. She was well known for her famous cheesecakes. Dave had a natural ability in the kitchen as well. His wife, Roberta, became the official taste tester. The family officially established September Farm Cheese in 2007 and each has made their mark on the cheese. Joy's Tomato Basil Jack cheese is named after Dave's mother and oldest daughter (also named Joy). Robertson's Select Cheddar derives its name from Dave's mother's maiden name. Pepperoni Augusto Jack incorporated the family name August (for Dave's grandfather, father, and Dave and Roberta's oldest son). Jumpin' Jack Jalapeño was named for Roberta's love of horses and jumping. Their Honey Brook Cheddar is named after the community of Honey Brook.

All in all, they are doing pretty well. Dave was named Chester County Farmer of the Year in 2013. After seven successful years of operating the cheese shop and production on the farm, they moved the business to its present location. They've designed and built a facility that resembles an old country store. The new building not only features the cheese manufacturing plant, but also offers a bakery, sandwich shop, and market.

Shellbark Hollow Farm, DAIRY, West Chester 19380; (610) 431-0786; shellbarkhollow@aol.com; shellbarkhollow.com. Shellbark Hollow Farm is nestled in the rolling hills of one of the most historic areas of the state. Not too far from Philadelphia or Valley Forge, they make award-winning artisan goat cheeses from their own herd of purebred Nubian goats. Cheesemaker Pete Demchur and his sister Donna Levitsky operate this family-run business, making handmade cheese onsite. The freshness of Shellbark Hollow Farm Cheese, typically less than a week old, speaks to the quality of their products. In the early 1970s, Pete found himself working with his sister's herd of Lamancha dairy goats. He fell in love with the animals and wanted to start his own herd. Later, when a friend mentioned she had two newborn goats, Pete's herd was "born". His herd and his cheesemaking grew from a hobby to a successful business selling cheese and goat products. Recognized as one of Chester County's oldest established artisan goat dairies, Shellbark Hollow Farm provides award-winning products to many chefs, fine restaurants, retail establishments, and local farmers' markets throughout the tri-state area. Shellbark Hollow Farm's herd of Nubian goats produces high-quality, rich, butterfat milk that cheese lovers crave. *Philadelphia* magazine honored Shellbark Hollow Farm with a "Best of Philly 2008" award for their Dry Sharp Chèvre, and the *Philadelphia Inquirer* named their Chèvre and Sharp 2 cheeses "Cheese of the Month" for November 2009. Shellbark Hollow Farm is a member of the Pennsylvania Association for Sustainable Agriculture, the Chester County Cheese Artisans, and the Pennsylvania Farmstead & Artisan Cheese Alliance. Onsite cheese sales by appointment only. Tours of the dairy are not available. See their website for a list of places where their cheese is sold.

Victory Brewing Company, BREWERY, 420 Acorn Lane, Downingtown 19335; (610) 873-0881; victorybeer.com. Open Mon through Sat, 11 a.m. to midnight; Sun, 11 a.m. to 10 p.m. Victory Brewing Company (VBC) was created by school bus buddies Bill Covaleski and Ron Barchet in 1996. Not that the two were always getting into trouble; the truth is, they make a great team. And they're looking forward to celebrating their 20th year in the beer and ale business. Set in an old

Pepperidge Farm factory, this brewery specializes in the British method of brewing, which is ironic since the British weren't too welcome here in the 1770s. But just ask the folks about the Great British Beer Festival of 2002. Beers from Victory Brewing Company were welcomed and then some. The brewery won for their Victory Hop Devil as Domestic Beer of the Year. They also produce ales, lagers, wheat beer, IPAs, stouts, and summer and winter seasonal beers. Victory churns out up to 100,000 barrels annually, and their beers are distributed in 34 states. They have developed a unique set of fans—the four-legged kind. Inspired by the dog days of summer, the pooch who's voted best looking in his or her Victory Brewing Company wear or simply looks so cute, graces the VBC's website.

The Woodlands at Phillips, MUSHROOMS, 1020 Kaolin Rd., Kennett Square 19348; (610) 444-2192; thewoodlandsatphillips.com. Open Mon through Fri, 10 a.m. to 4 p.m.; Sat, 10 a.m. to 3 p.m. The Woodlands is located in Kennett Square, "The Mushroom Capital of the World." The Phillips family invites locals and visitors to stop and explore the serene setting of the surrounding landscape and tour the pristinely restored home. The Woodlands home was built in 1828 and was acquired by the Phillips family in 1890. The renovations to the home reinstated the charm of the original construction. The store exterior features natural stone, pastoral brick, and vibrant red siding; the interior is warm and inviting. Rustic wood accents and artwork complement the earthy color palette, while ceramic pieces and kitchen accessories celebrate the uniqueness of the mushroom. They offer free mushroom cooking demonstrations in their modernized farmhouse kitchen and have a free mushroom-

growing exhibit and museum, where you can learn at your own pace how a third-generation family mushroom business grows mushrooms. You can actually see the mushrooms growing. The Woodlands stocks a wide assortment of fresh, dried, and jarred mushrooms daily. If you are looking to quickly spice up a meal or browse authentic mushroom recipes, stop in the store. There's a diverse selection of gourmet soup mixes and sauce packets always available, and the Phillips' recipes are shared.

Clarion

Briar Hill Rustic Furniture, FURNITURE, 4169 Route 36, Leeper 16233; (866) 744-9913; briarhillfurniture.com. Open Tues through Fri, 10 a.m. to 5 p.m.; Sat, 10 a.m. to 4 p.m.; Sun, noon to 4 p.m. The Briar Hill Rustic Furniture (est. 1952) facility is sandwiched between the scenic Allegheny National Forest and Cook Forest State Park in northwestern Pennsylvania. The surroundings have certainly inspired the father-and-son team of Denny and Allen Pierce—dynamic duo of rustically designed furniture. Stop by and you'll get to see "the place with the big swing" (a large stand-alone bench swing). Because Briar Hill offers both indoor and outdoor furniture, they allow customers the opportunity to customize their homes inside and out. They've got lots of choices, from deck and patio furniture to dining rooms and bedrooms. Briar Hill also has a selection of stains and finishes. Believe it or not, they recommend adding a "sunscreen'" stain to their outdoor furniture to maintain the color of the wood. They typically use Pennsylvania white pine for table and bench tops and white cedar for outdoor pieces, like the big swing.

Jeffrey McCombie Fine Art, BOWS, Clarion 16214; (814) 226-6834; jeffmccombie.com. Visits by appointment. Jeff McCombie's work has been exhibited at fine galleries in South Carolina, Arizona, and Pennsylvania. He's listed on the artist registry for the Bellefonte Art Museum. He's received many compliments about the balance and artistry of his work, but when he tells people that what they are actually looking at are humble little gourds, they walk away. A squash as an art form? Inconceivable! But that reaction is expected. Decorated hard shell gourds are said to be one of the oldest art forms, dating back some 5,000 years. Early on, artists discovered the beauty and function that this mundane medium provided.

As a confessed gourd-whisperer, Jeff happily listens to the squash speak to him to determine just what it should become. His journey began 20 years ago when he spent time in the Andes of South America. Decorated gourds were on display at festivals, museums, and galleries. He saw them back in the US as well. Upon retirement from his career in public education, Jeff began to explore the variety of textures and colors. Often the gourds he uses are grown in Lancaster. Each gourd is carefully selected after a yearlong drying process and cleaned to remove dirt and debris. Each gourd is sanded as many as eight times to obtain the perfect canvas. A variety of carving and burning techniques is incorporated to create each piece. He uses his own dyeing processes to create the beautiful layers of colors. And he may use metallic leafing or glazing techniques so his pieces resemble the rich finish of wood, the satiny smoothness of leather, or the sheen of brushed metal.

Stoke Hole Pottery, CERAMICS/POTTERY, 841 Reams Rd., Indiana 15701; (724) 541-3205; potterstour/stokehole.htm. Gallery is year-round and operates on an honor system; call ahead for appointments. Debra and Birch Frew are two potters who couldn't be happier when things get muddy. Debra was a ceramics instructor at Indiana University of Pennsylvania. It's rare to meet a teacher who practices what she preaches, but she is a full-time artisan. She's got a business, is raising two daughters, teaches pottery classes, and, oh yeah, owns a Great Dane because she likes to live life big. She loves to teach and likes to say that there are many glazes to suit your personal style and other materials to create a masterpiece essentially out of a ball of earth. Birch feels that his love of pottery is rooted in the belief that the production of functional ware, when transformed through the happy accidents of atmospheric firings, brings a mystical element to the daily rituals of life that are increasingly threatened by the society's fast food and paper plate mentality. He too has a love of teaching that stems from the desire to share his knowledge of, and enthusiasm for, clay with others.

Clearfield

Daniel McCombie Metal Work, METALWORKS, **1985 Beaver Run Rd., Westover 16692; mccombie4@hotmail.com.** Born in the Appalachian Mountains of western Pennsylvania, Daniel McCombie had metal in his blood. As a boy he hung out in his father's metal shop, watching in amazement as his dad cut, welded, heated, and bent iron. Daniel simply enjoyed boot stomping the sparks his father made in the process of hammering the metal. Daniel didn't fall in love with iron immediately, however, and admits that it wasn't until he became a young man that he appreciated the artistry he had been witnessing. Eventually he became a pipe fitter and steel fabricator. When he turned 26, he built his home on a ridge top with the Susquehanna River at its base. He'd been working as a therapist at a local hospital for many

years, but the desire to work with iron returned. Within six months, he had built a forge and attended classes in blacksmithing at Touchstone Center for the Arts. When Daniel has his irons in the fire, the smells take him back to his youth. The magic begins when he retrieves the glowing metal from the coals of the forge and then hammers his design on the edge of the anvil.

Wickett & Craig of America Tannery, LEATHER, 120 Cooper Rd., Curwensville 16833; (814) 236-2220 or (800) TANNERY; wickett-craig.com. Visitors are welcome; call ahead to make arrangements. Imagine a company that actually moves to the US intead of leaving. Wickett & Craig of America Tannery's 180,000-square-foot facility does all sorts of leather processing in an environmentally responsible fashion. From Toronto, Ontario, to the rolling hills of Clearfield County, they sell their leather to saddle and baggage companies as well as individual artisans who handcraft their own pieces. The company is serious about its leather. They do all sorts of "green" tanning, including Veg-tanning. Although an old process, it certainly is one that's less damaging to the environment. Tannins are chemicals naturally present in tree bark and leaves (vegetable matter). Animal hides are stretched and then left to soak in vats of different concentrations of tannin until they become supple—but are still strong and durable. Veg-tanned hides are often used in the making of furniture and luggage.

By the early decades of the 20th century, the tanneries of northern and western Pennsylvania had come to be generally owned by large companies that operated more than one plant. These included companies such as the United States Leather Company, Howes Brothers, Horton Crary and Company, and meat-packing giant Armour. These firms and other smaller-size ones processed 600,000 hides annually. By 2000, in spite of the closure of many of the state's tanneries and the overall decline of the industry throughout the nation, Pennsylvania remained the nation's largest employer of tanners, with over 2,300 workers employed in the trade.

Clinton

Woolrich Company, APPAREL, 39 Boardman Dr., Woolrich 17779; (800) 966-5372; woolrich.com. Open Mon through Sat, 9 a.m. to 5 p.m. Woolrich has been synonymous with warm, woolen outdoor clothing for more than 180 years. The company got its start in 1830 when John Rich, an English immigrant, built a wool mill in Plum Run. Rich took his wares to his customers, visiting the lumber camps that dotted the area. He sold all sorts of woolen items—socks, coverlets, and even yarn—from a mule cart. By 1845, he had built another mill a couple of miles up the road, near Chatham Run. Apparently, there was a steadier source of water. That second mill still exists today as part of the group of buildings, homes, and community establishments that have become Woolrich. Rich's woolen mills would withstand the Civil War, the Great Depression, two world wars, and the end of the Cold War. They would also witness the beginning of the Industrial Revolution in America, the expansion of American cities, and the telecommunications revolution. Woolrich is credited with pioneering the use of zippers in men's trousers, replacing buttons and ties. The Railroad Vest was introduced as railroads were being built through Pennsylvania, and it's still a popular item. Another garment with roots from the 1800s is the Buffalo Check Shirt that has kept many generations of outdoorsmen and women warm. And as America took to the roads in the early 1930s, Woolrich added automobile robes and steamer rugs for the more mobile society. Woolrich was contracted by the government to outfit Admiral Byrd's expeditions to Antarctica in 1939, 1940, and 1941. Eventually the introduction of new high-tech materials allowed Woolrich to enhance the performance of its outdoor wear, meeting the needs of a new generation of enthusiasts. Traditional fabrics such as wool and cotton teamed up with man-made fibers to create clothing that customers could rely on for everything from a backpacking trip to a leisurely stroll. Today the little village of Woolrich is still headquarters for the company, but the business has grown to a worldwide lifestyle company with a full range of outdoor-inspired products, from jackets and shirts to outdoor furniture. You can still buy a wool jacket your great-great grandfather may have worn in the woods or a parka that's incorporated the latest in advanced technology.

Columbia

Columbia County Bread and Granola, FOOD/BAKERY, 225 Center St., Bloomsburg 17815; (570) 441-4031; columbiacountybread.com. Open Mon through Sat, 8 a.m. to 4 p.m. This is not the kind of business you'd typically find near a college campus (Bloomsburg University is next door). The whole thing started with a tick bite, from which former New Yorker Doug Michael developed Lyme disease. He used nutrition to help his body heal from the disease, which often requires large doses of antibiotics. Handcrafted bread was his obsession for a long time. He wanted to offer it to the public, but he couldn't quite figure out how to make the whole thing work. He gave up several times but kept coming back to it. Once he moved to Bloomsburg, all the pieces fell into place. He moved operations to a refurbished Moose Lodge with a large commercial kitchen and large convection ovens. One year after making that move, Doug's granola was featured on the *Dr. Oz Show,* which was a boon for business for which he wasn't quite ready. The sales overwhelmed him, even in the larger kitchen. Then, just as he started looking for a new place, a fire destroyed the kitchen in the old Moose Lodge. Though he had insurance, he still lost about $50,000 in sales. Add to that loss the complications of working out of church kitchens and an Elks Lodge. Company morale sank.

His new space took more than six months to build. There were all kinds of approvals needed and myriad technical code issues. The team of bakers, all local guys, dug in with Doug and showed passion and an intuition for what needed to be done. At first, their best customers were diabetics. These days, the bakery is getting more gluten-sensitive customers. While their bread is technically not gluten-free, they prepare wheat for digestion through sprouting and fermentation. That seems to make all the difference. Columbia County Bakery bread can be eaten without

adverse reactions (weight gain, headaches, etc.) experienced with all other breads. If you can't stop in, their granola is available online from their website.

Susquehanna Glass, GLASS, 731 Ave. H, Columbia 17512; (717) 684-2155; susquehannaglass.com. Open Tues through Sat, 9 a.m. to 5 p.m. In 1910 Albert Roye installed a glass-cutting machine in a small shed behind his house and opened the Susquehanna Glass Factory. Two years later Albert's brother Walter joined the business. The operation grew and moved to its current location in Columbia, a stone's throw from the original shed where it all began. While hand-cutting glassware was the driving force behind the Roye's reputation for craftsmanship, they also incorporated new methods of decorating glassware. It added to the company's bottom line. Techniques such as sand etching, color screening, laser etching, and rotary engraving were added to increase the company's decorating repertoire. With these new decorating processes, the company was then able to add other media—metal, wood, acrylic, and leather—to its product line. Since 1797, when the central

Pennsylvania region's first two glasshouses opened, furnace stacks of glass factories were a standout of Pennsylvania's skyline. Dozens of glasshouses produced sheets of glass for a variety of uses around the nation and around the world. By the Civil War, the Pittsburgh region was regarded as the center of the nation's glass industry. About 50 years later Pittsburgh glass graced the walls of New York's transportation tunnels, the lights on the Panama Canal, and headlights for Ford automobiles. Happy to say Pennsylvania glass mugs were used in many a toast in beer halls and bars nationwide. Pennsylvania also produced glassware fine enough for five US presidents, and its stemware is present in embassies around the world.

Crawford

Campbell Pottery, CERAMICS/POTTERY, 25579 Plank Rd., Cambridge Springs 16403; (814) 734-8800; campbellpotterystore.com. Open daily, 10 a.m. to 5 p.m., March 1 to December 31. Closed Easter, Thanksgiving, and Christmas. Bill and Jane Campbell began their careers in the 1970s with two degrees in art and a strong desire to make practical art to use and enjoy every day. They began by showing and selling their work at craft fairs around the country, then selling to stores and galleries, eventually growing their studio into the largest art pottery in Pennsylvania. Now nationally recognized, Master Potter Bill Campbell has been creating award-winning porcelain for more than 40 years, specializing in functional work with elegant forms and rich glazes. In 1991 Bill and Jane decided to try a store of their own. With 500 galleries carrying their pottery and a staff of 20 to produce it, they took the plunge. They set up their craft show booths in the old tool shed of their barn as a test to see if people would come out to the country—and did they ever! The enthusiastic response fueled a dream that took 10 years to fully come true. Pottery lovers drive long distances to buy Campbell Pottery at the store (affectionately dubbed the "Mother Ship"). Bill still goes to the studio every day

and is excited about new ideas for forms and glazes, and anticipates opening the kilns and seeing each new firing.

Dad's Pet Food, PETS, 18746 Mill St, Meadville, PA 16335; (814) 724-7710; dadspetfood.com. In 1933 George Lang's Springer Spaniel had a litter of 11 puppies. Times were tough in 1933—the Great Depression made everything expensive, even commercial dog food. George made his own food and treats with an old peanut roaster. He began making dog food in earnest and called it DAD'S Health Wheat. He used locally milled grain and ground meat meal. The result was a dog biscuit and kibble that the dogs and puppies loved. The Lang family still owns and operates the plant. Their motto remains the same, "from farm to bowl." They're committed to making great-tasting pet foods that are wholesome and nutritious. They want you and your dog to be happy with the food. They're serious about quality. If you (or your pooch) are not completely satisfied with their products, just let them know and they'll gladly buy the package back. Who does that anymore? Dad's is available throughout the country, and you can find a retailer near you on their website.

Hare Today, PETS, 23556 Palmer Rd., Conneautville 16406; (800) 640-3582; hare-today.com. Open Mon through Thurs, 7 a.m. to 5 p.m.; Sat, 1 to 4 p.m. Please call ahead to schedule a visit. Whether you're looking for biologically appropriate raw food for your dogs, cats, ferrets, or reptiles, this is the place. Hare Today sells the most species-appropriate pet food you can buy. Tracy Murphy started her company as a small rabbitry. It's now a family-run, 52-acre farm where she raises rabbits, guinea pigs, goats, and more. Hare Today is licensed with the Pennsylvania Deptartment of Agriculture. It's inspected and registered with the US Food and Drug Administration. They've been in business since 1999. All poultry and fish are USDA-inspected and all-natural. Pork, beef, llama, and sheep are sourced from local farmers (no feed lot animals) and processed in a licensed state facility. All grinding, cutting, and packaging is done in their shop. Tracy deals with a lot of Amish neighbors and also two state-inspected local processing facilities, so you know there aren't any hormones, antibiotics, or preservatives added to the food she sells.

Cumberland

Caromal Colours, HOME DECORATING, 123 Main St., Mechanicsburg 17015; (717) 790-3190; caromalcolours.com. Open Mon through Fri, 9 a.m. to 5 p.m. Carol Kemery loves to watch paint dry. No, her life is not that boring, but this former ER nurse turned interior decorator creates her own line of paint that gives interiors and furniture new life by looking old. The distressed look that Carol teaches as a technique, gives all DIYers a feel for wall painting like no other. And watching it dry is as much fun as applying it to your walls, or furniture, or counter tops, or anything that's not moving. Her versatile paint process of layering tints, pigments, and finishes may involve more a than just a paintbrush, but it's not that hard. Carol demonstrates her technique at her classes, deftly applying base layer and textures. You can make your walls look aged with charm in an instant—something you can't get at a typical paint or home building supplies store. Carol began giving workshops to homeowners who wanted to create finishes in their own homes. She and her husband Al quickly realized that there were no products on the market that made this achievable. After a lot of product development and finding the best manufacturers, Caromal Colours was born. And yes, the name is a combination of their names, Carol M + Al.

Dan Hayward Art Glass, GLASS, 3 Appolossa Way, Carlisle 17013; (717) 877-9646. Visiting hours by appointment. Dan Hayward has worked in glass for more than 12 years, using traditional stained glass techniques (copper foil and lead "came") to create custom panels, windows, and other decorative objects. When developing patterns for stained glass, Dan often begins with a striking piece of art glass, then designs around its color and pattern. Other times he begins with a "found" object—say, a geode—and designs around that item. He likes to employ unique types of hand-formed art glass and

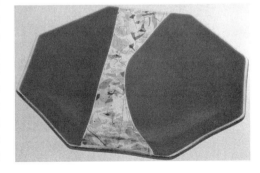

many varieties and textures of clear glass in his pieces. No two pieces are exactly alike, and all are notable for their clear edge around the central design. He also has three electric kilns where he creates functional fused glass. Dan likes to let the glass do the talking and allow the viewer to try to hear what it is saying. He describes his passion for glass as a great hobby of which he lost control—but he has no regrets. The fused glass process (or kiln-formed glass) requires heating the glass in a kiln to a temperature suitable for the result desired. Fused pieces typically have two layers: a clear base layer and the colored design layer. He cuts the pieces for the design layer, positions them on the base layer, and places the piece into a kiln. The kiln is heated to 1,475°F over several hours and then cooled back down through a controlled process called *annealing*. It takes about 12 hours before the glass is cool enough to handle. The resulting piece is then put on a clay mold, placed back in the kiln, and heated to 1,225°F. This is enough for the weight of the soft, but not molten, glass to "slump" down into the mold.

Keswick Creamery, DAIRY, 114 Lesher Rd., Newburg 17240; (717) 423-7658; keswickcreamery.com. Hours are seasonal, so it's best to call ahead. There's nothing more beautiful than rolling pastures of green grass with grazing cows. Elvis would have loved this farm—and he would have loved the farm's Stilton cheese called Blue Suede Moo. About 40 years ago Susan and Bill Dietrich started farming. When the kids (Melanie and Mark) came back from college about 20 years ago, they started making their own aged raw milk cheeses and soft cheeses, like ricotta. Their cows, registered Jerseys, the ones with the soft brown coats and big brown eyes, are rotationally grazed to keep the land and the cows healthy. This isn't just a hobby, the Dietrich family is serious about their cheeses, which have won gold and bronze medals for their excellence. They also incorporate local beer (Tröegs) to "wash" the rinds of some of their cheeses. The flavor of the beer coats the cheese, making for a multilevel tasting experience. The washings with beer may be done on a weekly basis as the cheese ages to impart a malty flavoring. That's one lucky cheese. Check out their website for a list of stores that carry their products.

Meadowbrooke Gourds, GENERAL ARTISANS, 125 Potato Rd., Carlisle 17015; (717) 776-6029; mbgourds.com. Open Mon through Sat, 10 a.m. to 4 p.m. Ben Bear saw a gourd in New England and thought it was a cute idea to turn a sturdy squash shell into something functional. He wanted to grow his own goose gourds. This was such a little craft that no one really needed, but his products were bought as fast as he could grow and craft them. Then came 2008 and the depression/recession. Suddenly, Ben had to specialize, because there were fewer dollars available to be spent on arts and crafts. Employees chose to reduce their pay by 25 percent to avoid layoffs. It took a while to adjust and to realize that all their past successes would be history if they didn't learn how to constantly improve everything. The seasonally decorated gourds are a delightful addition to your holiday decor. Faces and motifs adorn their exterior. They also make birdhouses, shapes, and container art. Meadowbrooke Gourds was also featured on the television series *Dirty Jobs*.

Metalled With Jewelry, JEWELRY, Village Artisans Gallery, 321 Walnut St., Boiling Springs 17007; (717) 258-3256; metalledwith.com and villageartisans gallery.com. Inspired by nature and mementoes of days gone by, Richelle Dourte creates jewelry that can preserve a piece of Pennsylvania forever. Richelle often uses leaves from the trees native to Pennsylvania forests. Since there are 133 species of these trees, she's got a lot from which to choose! She compresses each leaf into delicate earrings and pendants. Tiny maple leaves are often hard to come by in the local woods. Richelle has to compete with Gypsy month caterpillars that have defoliated hundreds of thousands of acres of forest. These caterpillars are not native to Pennsylvania, but were introduced in Massachusetts. They became widespread as moth egg–infested orchard fruit and wood products were delivered all over the Eastern US. The moths have eaten their way from Maine to Michigan. They've even hitched a ride cross-country and were spotted in Oregon. Luckily, Richelle won't let the insects ruin the beauty of her designs and jewelry. She has an online catalog and can custom make certain items for you.

The Pennsylvania Bakery, FOOD/BAKERY, 1713 Market St., Camp Hill 17011; (717) 763-7755; pabakery.com. Open Mon through Fri, 6 a.m. to 7 p.m.; Sat, 6 a.m. to 5 p.m. Baking has been a very important part of the Schenk family since the early 20th century, when John Schenk first began the trade in Germany. Eager to take advantage of the land of opportunity, John Schenk and his wife Pauline packed their belongings, along with the Schenk's family recipes, and immigrated to the US in pursuit of the American dream. They later settled in Germantown, where Schenk's Bakery was opened in 1938. John and Pauline had three children, Ken, Carl, and Erna. Ken and Carl learned the trade, continued in their father's footsteps, and became bakers. Ken Schenk, Jr. later completed formal baking and pastry arts training at Dunwoody Institute in Minneapolis. In 1986, Ken and his bride Michelle opened The Pennsylvania Bakery at its Camp Hill location, where it has been owned and operated for more than 27 years. Their three daughters, Rachelle, Hillery, and Kendall also work in the bakery. In 1997, the bakery underwent an expansion that more than doubled the size of the baking and retail operation. The Pennsylvania Bakery has passed down their recipes for five generations. In a day and age where many bakeries focus on a limited product line, they consider themselves a full-line bakery, offering a wide variety of specially decorated cakes for all occasions, European pastries, breakfast items, pies, cupcakes, cookies, and a full coffee shop. All their products are made from scratch and on the premises.

Dauphin

Appalachian Brew Company, BREWERY, 50 N. Cameron St., Harrisburg 17101; (717) 221-1080; abcbrew.com. Open Sun through Thurs, 11 a.m. to 11 p.m.; Fri and Sat, 11 a.m. to midnight. Tastings, Sat, 1 p.m. Old is good. Buildings, brewing methods, traditions—all of it. The original ABC Brewery is located in a brick building that dates to 1890. The brewery has been producing beer for 50 years. They expanded to include locations in Collegeville, Lititz, Gettysburg, Mechanicsburg, and Camp Hill. The brewery produces traditional ales, IPAs, lagers, wheat beers, bocks, and a chocolate stout that's as good as dessert. ABC also brews seasonal specials that make fall and winter something to look forward to in chilly Pennsylvania. ABC has reached out to non-imbibers as well by making sodas. Appalachian Craft Soda is a small-batch, carbonated beverage brewed using natural ingredients. And they even use natural sweeteners like pure cane sugar, stevia (a naturally sweet herb), and honey. They love beer very much and weren't too happy to discover that native Pennsylvanian Ben Franklin never said: "Beer is proof that God loves us and wants us to be happy." In fact, Ben disliked and complained about the early colonial habit of having a quick breakfast of heavily malted beer. Clearly, Ben never sipped an ABC brew.

Hershey's Chocolate World, CANDY/CHOCOLATE, 251 Park Blvd., Hershey 17033; (800) 468-1714; thehersheycompany.com. Open year-round, 9 a.m. to 9 p.m. Hershey's chocolate production has expanded exponentially since the turn of the century when Milton S. Hershey opened his factory doors. Today visitors to Hershey, the Sweetest Place On Earth, can experience what it's like inside a chocolate factory. Visitors can take a tour ride through a simulated factory at Hershey's Chocolate World Attraction, a candy-filled destination that has sweet adventures for everyone from chocolate lovers to fun seekers, shoppers, and history buffs.

The company originated with the candy-maker's decision in 1894 to produce sweet chocolate as a coating for his caramels. In 1900, the company began

producing milk chocolate in bars, wafers, and other shapes—and milk from the surrounding farms was plentiful. With mass production, Hershey was able to lower the per-unit cost and make milk chocolate, once a luxury item for the wealthy, affordable to all. One early advertising slogan described this new product as "a palatable confection and a most nourishing food." Looking to expand its product line, the company began producing a flat-bottomed, conical milk chocolate candy called Hershey's Kisses Chocolates in 1907. At first, they were individually hand-wrapped in little squares of silver foil, but in 1921, machine wrapping was introduced. That technology was also used to add the familiar "plume" at the top to signify to consumers that this was a genuine "Kiss." The candy even went to war. Named "Field Ration D," it was so successful that by the end of 1945, about 24 million bars were being produced every week. More successful still was their

Tropical Chocolate Bar, a heat-resistant bar with an improved flavor developed in 1943. In 1971, this same bar went to the moon with Apollo 15.

Hershey's Chocolate World exhibits and shops are now located across the globe from Las Vegas to Chicago to Niagara Falls to Dubai to Singapore. HersheyPark, a 120-acre theme park with more than 70 rides and attractions, was originally opened as a park for employees only, because Milton Hershey wanted his employees to have a place to relax and play with their families.

Hershey Violins, MUSICAL INSTRUMENTS, 11 West Main St., Mechanicsburg 17055; (717) 697-6341; hersheyviolins.net. Open Tues through Fri, 11 a.m. to 5 p.m.; Sat, noon to 3 p.m. Scott Hershey (yes, that's his real name) has been restoring and creating stringed instruments for 28 years. He's made over 100 violins. That's over five each year. Hershey Violins also offers the music lover a how-to class where you can actually make your own violin. You begin with a prefinished violin outfit for easy building. Seven three-hour, hands-on evening classes are taught, with the last class devoted to the playing of all completed instruments by a professional musician for tonal critique. A craftsmanship evaluation is also performed at this time. This is an aggressive program that will give the craftsman a better understanding of the violin-making process. The end result will be a beautiful, hand-varnished work of art. But Scott will also build one for you, in case you're more of an observer and the thought of building your own seems too daunting.

Just Four Dogs, PETS, 241 Audubon Dr., Harrisburg 17111; (717) 756-7519; justfourdogs.com. Open Mon through Fri, 9 a.m. to 9 p.m. Just Four Dogs is a bakery for dogs. It's a, well, barkery. But Just Four Dogs is kind enough to offer cat treats under their Just Four Cats product line. They will even custom make treats if your BFF (best furry friend) has special dietary needs. The barkery started with a German Shepherd puppy who had so many quirks that owner Maryann Geiman spent more time at home than at work. Maryann and her friend, Tesha, made dog treats with their kids one afternoon using a recipe they found in a magazine. It was fun and their dogs loved them (the kids, not so much). At her work, Maryann discovered her position was being eliminated. She spoke with her boss and both agreed that she'd be voluntarily laid off without the possibility of being called back. Her second puppy was six months old at the time. When she told Tesha that she was laid off, she asked, "Now what I am I going to do?" Tesha responded, "Let's sell dog treats!" She wasn't joking. The two started creating their first recipes and booked their first craft event, but found out they needed a license, treats tested, and a lot more. They cancelled. Both felt defeated. Yet, Maryann's husband was her biggest cheering section, encouraging her at every move. They gave it a go again and opened their first website and online store. In August 2013 Tesha moved to the Philadelphia area and has since started selling treats there. Their biggest joy is seeing the smiling dog faces and wagging tails of happy customers. Along the way they've made a ton of recipes and perfected their techniques for making the treats last without using preservatives. With all the dog food and treat recalls, it's nice to know that Just Four Dogs' dog treats are safe.

Little Owls Knit Shop, KNITTING, 2209 Paxton Church Rd., Harrisburg 17110; (717) 737-6700; littleowlsknitshop.com. Open Tues through Sat, 10 a.m. to 5 p.m. Made up of a quartet of women who want to share their love of the woven with the next generation and beyond, Little Owls Knit Shop is open to all ages, 8 to 88. Learn the basics of knitting in as little as three hours. You and your child can even begin your first project together. You'll learn how to do the knit stitch and purl stitch, how to cast on and bind off, and gain tips on reading patterns.

Beth Kurtz began knitting when she became an empty nester. Her journey into all things fiber has been fearless, and she will knit anything. What's the worst that can happen after all? Just rip it out and start again. Beth loves trying new knitting techniques, learning new skills, and experimenting. Spending time with other knitters is also a favorite of hers, as she feels they are some of the nicest people.

Kristin Runyon is a former K-2 librarian and mother of two spunky little girls. She first picked up the needles in college and has never looked back. After getting married she realized her true calling was casting on and binding off as her initials spell knitter (KNTR).

Michelle Eichelberger is an equal opportunity crafter, but knitting is her greatest passion. When she began knitting, socks were (and still are) her go-to project. Over the years her creativity has grown from shawls to spinning with a drop spindle. She is always finding ways to challenge herself with new techniques and patterns.

Rachel Lightner is a mother of three, ages six and under, and knitting has saved her sanity. She started knitting before her first child was born, and hasn't stopped. The four ladies' knitting motto: There's always something new to learn.

Rainbow Vision Stained Glass, GLASS, 3105 Walnut St., Harrisburg 17109; (717) 657-9737; rainbowvisionsg.com. Open Mon and Thurs, 10 a.m. to 8 p.m.; Wed and Fri, 10 a.m. to 5 p.m.; Sat, 9 a.m. to 3 p.m.; Sun, noon to 3 p.m. The outside of this establishment looks like a turn-of-the-century house. A wrap-around porch, an unremarkable white exterior, and a rather innocuous sign would lull you into thinking there's not much to see. Go inside and your whole view of color changes. You will indeed find a rainbow of shiny, opaque, and colorful glass. Even if you dabble in the stain glass or mosaic art, you will find your needs met. Rainbow Vision stocks over 400 styles and colors of glass—and in varied thicknesses too. You can buy clear beveled glass or deep blue, rippled glass. They have tools and classes to guide you through each step. You can even select a gift from their shop and have it shipped to your home. Sometimes it's best to let the professionals pack their own glass. Rumor has it that Rainbow Vision has industrial-strength bubble wrap. It's more likely they have perfected the technique of safely wrapping their products.

Tröegs Brewery, BREWERY, 200 E. Hersheypark Dr., Hershey, 17033; (717) 534-1297; troegs.com. The General Store is open Mon through Sat, 11 a.m. to 8 p.m.; Sun, 11 a.m. to 5 p.m. The tasting room is open Sun through Wed, 11 a.m. to 9 p.m.; Thurs through Sat, 11 a.m. to 10 p.m. Tröegs Brewery was founded in 1996 by brothers John and Chris Trogner. Tröegs is combination of their last name and the Flemish word *Kroeg*, meaning "pub." Their first keg was sold at a Harrisburg restaurant on July 18, 1997. (The guys remember that date—their wedding anniversaries, not so much.) Tröegs Brewery was situated in Harrisburg until 2011, when they moved operations to Hershey, where all beer production now takes place. You can still check out the old location, (now a Habitat For Humanity furniture store) to see where it all started. Tröegs Brewery is unique in the beer arena because they produce what they call Scratch Beers. These brews are part of their research and development. They're brewed in limited, small batches and available only at the brewery. While every Scratch Beer that's released can be found on tap in their tasting room, not all are bottled. They are strictly brewery-only releases. Occasionally, you may find Scratch Beers on tap at special events such as Tap Takeovers or Pint Nights throughout their distribution footprint. But you may have to make the trip to Hershey to sample these one-of-a-kind beers. Just think of being the luckiest guinea pig in the world.

Delaware

George Morris Wood Turning, WOODWORKING, Upper Darby 19082; gmorris465@gmail.com; georgemorriswoodturnings.com. When a firefighter retires you'd figure he'd want to stay far away from anything even remotely flammable. But not George Morris; he loves wood—cherry and maple and lots of it. Sure, he'll make the typical bowls and hollow forms, but his standout creations are his assorted saltshakers and pepper mills. With a plain wood finish or a dash of bright fire engine red, these kitchen utensils are sturdy, yet whimsical. Ergonomically shaped, but also revealing the wood's charming imperfections, they are the product of a solid, yet creative person. Because pepper loses its flavor through evaporation, airtight storage is essential. And it can lose some of its flavor when exposed to light, so leave those clear plastic peppermills in the store. Pepper mills originated in France in the 1840s. Up until then, most people used a mortar and pestle to crush the peppercorns. The pepper mill design was, in part, inspired by the giant millstones, large stones that turned and crushed or ground seeds to make meal or flour. The pepper mill funnels

It's a Pennsylvania Thing

Hires Root Beer, Philadelphia 19112. Hires Root Beer was created by Philadelphia pharmacist Charles Elmer Hires. The official story is that Hires first tasted root beer, a traditional American beverage dating back to the Colonial era, while on his honeymoon in 1875. However, historical accounts vary and the actual time and place of the discovery may never be known. By 1876 Hires had developed his own recipe and was marketing 25-cent packets of powder that each yielded five gallons of root beer. At Philadelphia's Centennial Exposition in 1876, he cultivated new customers by giving away free glasses of root beer. Hires marketed it as a solid concentrate of 16 wild roots and berries. It claimed to purify the blood and make rosy cheeks. In 1884 he began producing a liquid extract and a syrup for use in soda fountains, and was soon shipping root beer in kegs and producing a special fountain dispenser called the Hires Automatic Muni-maker. In 1890 the Charles E. Hires Company incorporated and began supplying Hires root beer in small bottles, claiming to have sold over a million bottles by 1891. Consolidated Foods bought the company from the Hires family in 1960, only to sell Hires 2 years later to Crush International. Procter & Gamble bought Crush in 1980, and sold it to Cadbury Schweppes in 1989. Cadbury divested its soft drinks arm in 2008, and the beverage company renamed itself Dr Pepper Snapple Group that year.

Harley-Davidson (Motorcycle), York 17402. Established as an assembly parts facility in 1973, the site is now a museum and a mecca for all Harley-Davidson lovers. It all began in 1903 when youngsters William S. Harley, 23, and Arthur Davidson, 22, offered the first Harley-Davidson motorcycle. The pair built the contraption in a 10-by-15-foot wooden shed with the words "Harley-Davidson Motor Company" scrawled on the door. The first Harley-Davidson dealer opened in Chicago in 1904 and the first Harley factory was built in Milwaukee in 1906. In 1918 Harley helped the World War I effort by manufacturing 20,000 motorcycles.

James Industries, Hollidaysburg 16648. In 1943 three men in Philadelphia (Richard James, Coleman Barber, and Dylan Gedig) observed a torsion spring fall off a table and roll around on the deck at the Cramp shipyards in Philadelphia. Thinking there could be a toy in this, the three men borrowed $500, experimented with materials, ran tests, and produced 400 units of the toy. Richard's wife Betty James came up with the name "Slinky." In 1945 Richard and Betty James were granted permission to set up an inclined plane in the toy department at Gimbels in Philadelphia to demonstrate the Slinky's battery-less "walking" abilities. In 1948 they built a factory in suburban Philadelphia for James Industries' 20 employees. Ten years later headquarters were set up in Hollidaysburg, where the factory remained for 30 years.

K'Nex Toy Company, Hatfield 19440. Sometimes the greatest ideas spring from boredom. K'Nex Toy Company Founder Joel Glick was at a noisy, crowded wedding reception, bored to tears, when he began playing with those little drink straws. Then he began building with them, inserting one into the other and then bending another. Then he began dreaming of the possibilities. With a little product engineering, in 1992 he completed the building system of rods and connectors. Later he added wheels, pulleys, and gears to make vehicles, roller coasters, and as-large-as-your-dream-is creations. The company has expanded to include all sorts of building sets. They acquired Tinkertoy (the Hasbro brand created in 1913 by Pajeau, Pettit, and Tinker) and the famous Lincoln Logs (created in 1916 by John Lloyd Wright). All K'Nex toy parts are made in Pennsylvania by the Rodon Group (an eco-friendly plastics manufacturing company). In keeping with the toy makers' innovative lead, there are online options for expanding your construction universe, contests, and challenges. And, for those of us who didn't read the directions, online help.

Quinn Flags, 581 West Chestnut St., Hanover 17331; (717) 634-2147 or (800) 353-2468; quinnflags.com. This flag company is one of the newer flag companies in Pennsylvania—it's a mere 11 years old. However this flag company has been successful in making historical flags and buntings. They also help customers create flags or banners according to personal specifications. They manufacture custom flags, banners, display hardware, pennants, and windsocks. Quinn Flags is the parent company of Promo Flag Maker. They specialize in quick turnaround for all imprinted knit polyester flags, banners, pennants, and more. They'll go as small as little stick flags for your interior decor and as big as large stadium banners for professional sporting venues.

Vintage Shoe Company (HH Brown), Martinsburg 16662. You know you've arrived when celebrities are wearing your stuff. That's the case for a shoe company that insisted on designing and handmaking shoes and now is the only domestic shoe company that makes its own wares, seen on celebrities such as Aaron Paul (*Breaking Bad*), Brice Butler (Oakland Raiders), and Taylor Swift (who's Pennsylvania made, thank you very much). While the factory was built in the 1950s, HH Brown became involved in the 1970s. They make all kinds of shoes, but their forte is leather boots. Under the HH Brown Shoe Company umbrella, the Cove brand makes boots for police officers and the military. Brands Vintage and Walk Over take some of the most iconic styles of the past century and re-create them. The vintage-inspired designs are authentic to the last grommet. One of their most poignant replicas is called the Paratrooper "Jump Boot." During World War II, airborne forces landed behind enemy lines via airplanes and parachutes. Their combat footwear were sturdy, ankle-supporting, lace-up boots. Today, for the civilians, HH Brown offers loafers, oxfords, chukkas, and sturdy and casual boots in soft suede and supple leather.

the peppercorns into grooves. They are then rubbed against an inner grate that cracks and grinds them into the powder that makes you sneeze. If you're not a fan of pepper, George also has salt mills to help grind your chunky sea salt.

Pet Bistro, PETS, 202 W. Lancaster Ave., Ste. 248, Wayne 19087; (610) 937-6200; petbistro.us. Pet Bistro is an organic dog food company that specializes in organic dog treats. And with names like Organic Bark-Scotti how can you resist? This dog food company uses a holistic approach to dog health that's rooted in the application of phytomedicine. That's the herbal-based practice that uses various plant materials that are considered both preventive and therapeutic. It's like having an herbalist for your dog. Pet Bistro uses organic whole (non-GMO) foods that contain natural medicinal properties. It's common sense that you can maintain the health of your dog through nutritious whole food consumption. All the good stuff is here—organic vegetables, grains, fruits, and herbs. They use no animal by-products, toxic chemicals, preservatives, pesticides, hormones, antibiotics, or artificial ingredients—they believe in their product so much they are willing to give you a free sample. Company president Rafaela Miett may seem a little over the top in his passion for providing as pure a food as he possibly can for your dog, but he loves what he does. Skin allergies are one of the main reasons people bring their pets to the vet. Skin is, in essence, your pet's barometer of health. And if your pet consumes all-natural pet food, chances are, his or her body will be healthy and his or her skin will show it. Pet Bistro products are available at specialty pet shops throughout the country.

Elk

Joseph Wortman Wood, WOODWORKING, 219 Badeau Rd., Kersey, PA 15846; (814) 834-1989. Call ahead for studio hours. Joseph Wortman started woodworking by building houses as a hobby. It was the cabinet making he enjoyed the most and was the best at. For the most part he's self-taught with a few classes thrown in. He confesses that he's found finishing projects primarily from wood to be both relaxing and challenging, but also rewarding. Studies have proven Joseph correct. Stress management research has shown that individuals who engage in relaxing hobbies or pastimes have lower blood pressure and are better able to recharge their batteries to face the chaos of life than those who don't. When Joseph wanted to expand his woodworking beyond cabinetry, he turned to the Artisan Trail (a group of artisans in Pennsylvania). They are able to promote and support his passion for wood. Furniture and wooden chests and boxes are another direction Joseph plans to pursue. Most of the wood for the projects is grown, harvested, sold, and worked in the Pennsylvania Wilds Artisan Trail website (pawildsartisans.com).

SDAJ (Stephanie Distler Artisan Jewelry), JEWELRY, 300 Mill St., Johnsonburg 15845; (814) 512-1209; stephaniedistler.com. The studio is open year-round, call ahead for appointments. Stephanie Distler doesn't have to choose between working outside or having an office job—she gets both. She works out of a home-based garden studio. Stephanie admits she's self-taught and has never taken a formal course in metalwork. Still, she doesn't let that stop her from doing metal filigree and metal printing with designs stamped to create sayings for businesses,

weddings, personal mantras, family pendants, and more. Her designs include hand-created closures, earwires, beads, and other unique components combining art and function. Her metal techniques include soldering, fusing, metal printing, cold connections, pounded-out wire grommets, hammer forging, and wire wrapping. A variety of metal finishing techniques is added to the metal-smithing process. Stephanie has three daughters, and her metalwork has done two things for her family. First, it gave her a way to stay home to raise her children, and second, she was able to keep in touch with her creative passion. Inspired by her surroundings, she loves how the natural environment can emerge from her hand tools and hammer. Her daughters now take part in the artisanal work. Stephanie notes that when you have a love or passion, it spills out around you. It's contagious joy. And that creative joy brings people closer.

Straub Brewery, BREWERY, 303 Sorg St., St. Mary's 15857; (814) 834-2875; straubbeer.com. Tours are given Tues and Wed at 10:30 a.m.; Thurs and Fri at 10:30 a.m. and 12:30 p.m., and on Sat by appointment only. There's an old photo of the brewery's founder Peter Straub at the brewery. The face staring out at you looks a little, well, scary. But never judge a book by its cover, or a beer by the brewmaster's expression. Straub, born in a small town in Germany, was originally trained as a cooper (barrelmaker) before he immigrated to Pennsylvania in 1869. Only 19 at the time, he began work in a brewery—he would work in four (technically five) before he started his own. In 1872, Straub went to work as a brewmaster for Luhr Brewery, but didn't own the brewery until 1878. He then renamed it Straub and Sons Brewery. Since then, this family-owned brewery has been ahead of the curve, avoiding a shutdown during Prohibition by making near-beer (less alcohol than regular beer). They have also never used preservatives in their brewing process. One of things this clever cooper-turned-brewmeister implemented was putting a red metal ring around the barrels or kegs of his beer. That way his customers knew they were drinking Straub beer, and he was always able to get the barrels back. Today, you'll still see the red ring around the Straub beer kegs as a nod to the forward-thinking Straub.

Erie

Erie Brewing Company, BREWERY, 1213 Veshecco Dr., Erie 16501; (814) 459-7741; eriebrewingco.com. Tours are offered Wed through Fri, noon to 5 p.m.; Sat, 1 to 4 p.m. More than 20 years of brewing, 11 different kinds of beer and ale (not including seasonal brews), and distribution to over a dozen states—that's some successful suds. The Erie Brewing Company (EBC) was originally founded as Hoppers Brewpub in the historic Union Station. The station was founded in 1851, revamped in 1866, and received an art

deco facelift in 1927. EBC churns out about 6,000 barrels of beer annually. Not bad for a brewery that has to tough out winters on Lake Erie. The 2014 record snowfall was over nine feet. Hint: Try their Mad Anthony's American Pale Ale, named after General Anthony Wayne of the American Revolutionary War. Rumor has it that during the war he was shot so many times that he developed a "madness" from lead poisoning caused by all the lead bullets in his body (which isn't true). He died in 1796, and was buried in Erie only to be dug up years later by his angry son, upset that his father had not been buried in the family plot at St. David's Churchyard in Valley Forge (about 280 miles away). His son ignored directives not to drive angry and rode so fast that many of the General's bones fell out of the wagon and were strewn all over Pennsylvania.

Flexcut Tool Company, WOODWORKING, 8105 Hawthorne Dr., Erie 16509; (814) 864-7855; flexcut.com. Founded in 1986 under the name of Falls Run Woodcarving, this shop was simply a wood-carving school. In 1992 Flexcut began manufacturing a new breed of wood-carving tools to address the needs of the modern hobbyist and professional. Wood-carving tools haven't changed much since the industrial revolution, but the people practicing wood carving have. Beginning with only four different tool profiles, Flexcut now produces and distributes over 300 products developed specifically for the wood-carving market. Chances are, your local hobby shop carries their brand. Over the last few years, they have introduced the Carvin' Jack Collection, folding jackknives that are designed for portable wood carving. They also developed sharpening products, called Micro Tools, which keep your knives from going dull—dull knives are one of the main reasons people cut themselves. You have to push harder on a dull blade than on a sharp one. Extra force often means you lose a little control. Even if you whittled a walking stick as a Boy (or Girl) Scout, or as a hobby, your hand probably touched a Flexcut tool. The brand is at the forefront of hobby blades. Products are available online or in your local crafting and hobby store.

Triple Creek Maple, MAPLE, 9225 Fillinger Rd., Cranesville 16410; (814) 756-4500; triplecreek@nwsd.org; triplecreekmaple.com. Visitors are welcome, call ahead for hours. Triple Creek Maple is proud to produce a high-quality product that every sweet tooth will love. Gary and Shirley Bilek have won awards at the Pa. Farm Show. Their maple syrup has an average of 67 percent sugar content, going over and above (in thickness and sweetness) what Pennsylvania law requires. They increase the percent of sugar by boiling the syrup longer, making it much thicker and more desirable. This process sometimes results in excess sugar crystals forming in the bottom of the container. You see this when you store your maple syrup in the fridge. No worries though, sugar crystals are simply a sign of a thick, quality syrup. The USDA recently adopted a new maple syrup grading system. Previously, syrup was either Grade A (lighter in flavor and typically poured on pancakes) or Grade B (darker and robust in flavor, great for cooking and baking). But people thought Grade B meant the syrup was inferior, when in fact, B-quality meant it was collected or tapped later in the season when conditions create a thicker consistency and deeper flavor. Now, all syrups are graded according to color—golden, amber, dark, and very dark. You can see and taste the differences for yourself.

Fayette

Youghiogheny Opalescent Glass, GLASS, 300 South 1st St., Connellsville 15425; (724) 628-305; youghioghenyglass.com. Open Mon through Fri, 9 a.m. to 2 p.m.; Sat, 9 a.m. to noon. The Youghiogheny Opalescent Glass gallery and retail store is located in the 1911 P&LE passenger station, a historic landmark. The art of stained glass dates back to ancient Phoenician sailors who, when shipwrecked on a sandy beach, lit a large fire for rescue purposes. The fire's heat melted the sand underneath. When it cooled, the hardened, clear "rock" was kept as a souvenir and the technique replicated. Glass was "invented." It was also used as an art form by the Greeks, Romans, and Arabians. The oldest example of European stained glass was in the St. Paul's Monastery in Jarrow, England, in 686 AD. And of course, stained glass reached western popularity during the medieval ages when churches large and small were adorned with these "glass gems."

Glass making (stained and clear) came to this part of Pennsylvania around the late 1700s. The factory and production setting of western cities like Pittsburgh made it possible to manufacture glass on a large-scale. The ornamental aspect was almost lost. But with artists such as Louis Tiffany, opalescent glass, which is translucent and light reflective, was pigment and canvas. Tiffany, although a New York native (we forgive him), left his glass mark on churches, banks, and mausoleums in this area. The Youghiogheny Opalescent Glass gallery has antique stained glass items as well as their own line of fine jewelry, kaleidoscopes, stemware, and paperweights

Franklin

Lone Oak Brooms, BROOMS, Amberson 17210; (717) 349-7979; BobHaffly@ embarqmail.com. Bob Haffly makes witches happy. Seriously, at a show where he was demonstrating his craft, a woman who described herself as a witch (Wiccan), requested one of Bob's handmade brooms, and she was delighted with her purchase. Bob says he hasn't seen her since. He considers that a good thing. Brooms and Pennsylvania have some history together. Benjamin Franklin is credited with introducing broomcorn to the US in the early 1700s. Initially, broomcorn was grown only as a garden crop. A type of sorghum, broomcorn produces heads with fibrous seed branches that may be as long as 36 inches—perfect for sweeping. Years ago, Bob caught auction fever and bid on (and won) two broom-making machines. He hauled them home and there they sat for months. Not having a clue about how to make brooms, he tried to sell the machines—no luck. Finally a friend asked, "How hard can it be to make a broom?" Bob taught himself and discovered there's a real demand for local, sturdy brooms (aside from the Halloween rush). Bob also makes ceremonial wedding brooms for a custom popular in African American and Irish American cultures in which a couple jumps over a broom together believing it will bring them luck.

Fulton

New Morning Farm, FARMS, 22263 Anderson Hollow Rd., Hustontown 17229; (814) 448-3904; newmorningfarm.net. Seasonal hours. Jim and Moie Crawford began growing organic vegetables, berries, and herbs on their New Morning Farm in 1972, before it was cool and before there was even a certification process. The farm was originally a dariy farm, but they managed with a lot of innovation and trial and error to turn it into an amazing organic farm. They undergo yearly inspections and are as transparent as a farm can be. They make sure they rotate crops—growing different crops in different fields each year so the soil is healthy and not depleted of nutrients. They have even inspired neighboring farms to go organic too. In the late 1980s the Crawfords formed a co-op called the Tuscarora Organic Growers Cooperative. Since then, they have generated about $3 million in sales. New

Morning Farm is now equipped for year-round production, thanks in part to three heated greenhouses and two high tunnel cold frames. There are also refrigerated coolers to keep produce fresher longer. They offer garlic, herbs, onions, beets, and carrots year-round, and seasonal produce such as lettuce, beans, raspberries, squash, and tomatoes. The Crawfords are so good at what they do, they have fans who buy from their satellite farmers' markets in Washington DC.

Greene

Westerwald Pottery, CERAMICS/POTTERY, 40 Pottery Ln., Scenery Hill 15360; (724) 945-6000; westerwaldpottery.com. Open Mon through Fri, 8:30a.m. to 4:30 p.m.; Sat, 10 a.m. to 4:30 p.m. No ordinary pottery guy, Phil Schaltenbrand is also a historian and professor. You might say he practices what he teaches. And he never lets a good challenge stand. In 1976 when he was asked to create some "appropriate" pieces for the nation's upcoming bicentennial, Phil stepped up to the plate, drawing on his knowledge of historic pottery and the nation's roots. He produced one-of-a-kind stoneware, hand-painted a lovely cobalt blue. The design of the pottery was so eye-catching that a year later Phil's thrown pottery barely sat on a shelf long enough to cool from the kiln. The first to use the cobalt blue brush decoration, he's not afraid of other colors and designs. His work is current and functional. His "sinkmates" are tilted crocks designed to hold pot scrubbers. He ensures each piece bears his stamp and signature. His book, *Big Ware Turners*, chronicles the history of Pennsylvania pottery in text and photos of antique pottery and crockware. The preservation of this functional and decorative art is essential to the preservation of the history of Pennsylvania because, as Phil knows, every piece of hand-thrown pottery tells its own story.

Indiana

Autumn House Farm, KNITTING, 1001 Locust Rd., Rochester Mills 15326; (724) 286-9596; autumnhousefarm.com. Under the watchful eye of Harriet Knox, knitters learn to cast on and bind off at Autumn House Farm. They talk about sheep, wool, and fleece. They discover the process of preparing yarn, from shearing to carding to spinning. And they often forge friendships as tight as their stitches. While much of the work is done by hand, Harriet has an on-site carding machine, which fluffs the wool prior to twining it into a useable (and recognizable) skein of yarn. She's proud of her farm, which has goats, sheep, and rabbits—all for the purpose of making something warm and wearable for you, by her or by you. Harriet has three different breeds of sheep and she'll be the first to tell you—not all fleeces are created equally. Different sheep breeds produce different wool, and even the same breed can produce thicker (or thinner) fleeces depending on the time of year. (October fleeces are especially prized.) If you're knitting an afghan, you should know that it can take up to three sheep to produce enough yarn to knit a wrap-around-you-during-a-football-game kind of throw. Autumn House has been open to the public for over 30 years and has been a true wool-working farm for over 40 years. Workshops, classes, and "fiber getaway weekends" are all facilitated on the farm, while guests comfortably stay overnight in the farm's guesthouse, which they rent out. Call for hours.

Jefferson

BWP Bats, SPORTING EQUIPMENT, 80 Womeldorf Lane, Brookville 15825; (814) 849-0089; bwpbats.com. Factory tours are offered Mon through Sat, 8 a.m. to 5 p.m. Groups of 8 or more must call ahead. The most serious baseball fans come out for the Little League Baseball World Series Championship, usually played near the end of August each year. Luckily, BWP is only a two-hour drive away from the League's Williamsport baseball fields, just in case an extra bat is needed. BWP, which stands for Brookville Wood Products, has been in the wood business for almost 50 years, but they have only been making bats since 1990. They manufacture wooden bats (primarily maple, oak, and birch) for professional and amateur baseball players, as well as for softball and T-ball. They also make commemorative bats customized to recall the date of your first home run. They sell wall mounts and bat holders to display "Mr. Nasty"—a real name of a BWP bat. Their customized process ensures that you will get the right bat for your swinging needs. They have several color and pattern options from which to choose should your little princess need a camo-pink softball bat. BWP makes more than 35,000 bats each year and welcomes over 20,000 visitors to tour their factory annually.

Cat's Eye Stained Glass, GLASS, 6594 River Rd., Sigel 15860; (814) 752-2432. Call ahead for studio hours. David Herring and his wife Melody are inspired by Tibet, their cat that supervises them in their studio. It's also the same feline that gave these artisans their business name. David has been working with stained glass for 28 years. His fascination with creating beautiful and colorful "pictures in glass" using the solid/liquid translucence of glass is reflected in his eclectic style. Nature has always influenced his work, whether he is creating a panel in a traditional Victorian, Craftsman, or art-deco style, or a natural scene. Dave was born in the Upper Peninsula of Michigan. His time spent there and summers in northern Minnesota gave him the run of the area's rivers, forests, and lakes. Several extended trips throughout the western states, the Yukon, British Columbia, and Alaska have also inspired his designs. Today, daily inspiration lies a few feet from his door. His home and Cat's Eye Stained Glass Studio is on the Clarion River surrounded by the Allegheny National Forest and state game lands.

The Open House Shop, FURNITURE, 265 Allegheny Blvd, Brookville 15825; (814) 849-5655. Open Sun through Thurs, noon to 5 p.m.; Fri through Sat, 10 a.m.

to 5 p.m. Robin Mullen-Park and her husband Charles create custom farm tables with wood from their area as well as vintage wood, reproducing the history of tables as they were used in earlier times. Their artistic style is primitive, and their products tie into both the farming and lumber traditions for which the region is known. The style, while primitive, is also simple, rustic, and functional. Charles is a wood finisher and general contractor (and has been for more than 30 years). Robin learned her finishing techniques from him and has progressed in her wood finishing talents. They work as a team, creating beautiful products that can be used throughout the home. They collect and carry unique folk art. And their shop also carries antiques and items that add to the primitive decor they love. The furniture paints and finishes are subtle and subdued. You won't find any headache-inducing bright yellows or greens. Their work is soothing and pleasant to the eye—and to the hand.

Windy Hill Farm Naturals, SOAPS, 10445 Route 28 North, Brockway 15824; (814) 328-5346; windyhillfarmnaturals.com. Hours are seasonal, so it's best to call ahead. Sherry Trunzo and her husband bought the farm in 1995. After a year's renovation, they moved into the farmhouse, established an organic vegetable garden, and started working the hayfields, which had been neglected for years. They were told hay would never grow on them again, but they are now supplying

hay to the horse owners in their area as well as growing for their own horses. They also sell their vegetables, fresh and dried herbs, and maple syrup at local farmers' markets and at several local restaurants. On a lark, Sherry decided to take a soap-making class from a local business (Quiet Creek School of Country Living in Brookville). After using the soap she made, she couldn't imagine going back to store-bought soap. She started making it for her family. It grew from there. The business seemed to just take off with everyone offering suggestions as to what to make next. A buyer at one of the stores suggested lotion bars, her grandchildren wanted lip balm, and a niece wanted fragrance diffusers. Sherry listened to everyone. She took suggestions from customers at the craft shows she attended. She did her best to make what her client base was asking for, while still keeping the naturally-made products that she thinks are so important to her and the environment. All of her products are available from the website and, if you're in the area, they're available at Brockway Farmer's Market held every Fri starting at 9 a.m. at the high school parking lot from late June through the end of September. All the soaps are hand-cut bars that are approximately four ounces. Sherry makes a cute little groundhog soap and other animal shapes for the kids because it can be fun to be clean.

Juniata

Hidden Treasures Originals by Kathy Graybill, FURNITURE/GENERAL ARTISANS, 6835 Route 75 South, East Waterford 17021; (717) 734-2307; graybills-hiddentreasures.com. Open by appointment or special event. Kathy and Jeff Graybill say their Tavern and Trade Signs are their number-one seller, but Kathy also paints decorated furniture, chests, and boxes. Most of their artistic renderings are one of a kind. They make a full line of reproduction boxes, candle boxes, pipe boxes, hanging cupboards, and signs. In addition, Kathy hooks rugs and creates folk sculptures. In the late 1990s, the Graybills started out doing small craft shows and street and craft festivals—all while working full-time jobs. They moved back to Lancaster after a three-year stint in Baltimore and decided to give sign painting a try full time. They've been featured in magazines such as *Early American Life* and *Primitive Place* magazine. When they sold out at their first trade show, they knew they could make a go of signs as a their only source of income. It's been tough, many days and nights on the road, travelling to shows, sometimes

25 a year. They are now down to doing only three shows and a few open houses per year. Their signs range in size, but all are painted free hand by Kathy, including the lettering and dates. The couple layers and mixes their own colors and uses a vinegar glaze, just like the original painters.

Lackawanna

My Kielbasa from Schiff's, MEAT, 3410 Main Ave., Scranton 18447; (570) 343-1295; mykielbasa.com or myschiffs.com. Open Mon through Sat, 7 a.m. to 9 p.m.; Sun, 7 a.m. to 6 p.m. This is the place to get this one-of-a-kind Polish sausage. In fact the word *kielbasa* is the general word for sausage in Polish. If you ask for kielbasa at a Polish butcher shop or store, they're likely to ask you which kind of kielbasa? Scranton was home to large populations of German, Irish, and Polish immigrants who left their homelands to come to Pennsylvania to work the land or in the coal mines and slate quarries in the mid-1800s. The Germans brought with them their love of food and their traditional meat-processing techniques and favorite sausage recipes. Most kielbasa is made up of about half pork and half beef. The meat mixture is spiced and cured. It can be eaten cold or cooked, often as a breakfast meat in place of bacon or sausage. You typically see it in rings and can buy it by the pound, unsliced. You can order online, or order and carryout at the shop.

Plumpy's Pierogies, PIEROGIES, 515 Delaware St., Jessup 18434; (570) 489-5520; facebook.com/Plumpys. Open Tues through Sat, 9 a.m. to 6 p.m. It was a recipe that started over 75 years ago with Mike Cortazar's great-grandmother. Today he makes over 12 different varieties and seasonal specials. Mike has stretched the family recipe list to include more than a dozen varieties of signature pierogies. He also makes and sells some of Poland's other great dishes such as *haluski* (cabbage and noodles), *latkes* (potato pancakes), and *pagash* (a combination of pizza and mashed potatoes, traditionally eaten during Lent). From traditional potato and sauerkraut, to the more adventurous blueberry or portabella mushroom pierogies, Plumpy's makes more than 300 dozen of the stuffed-dough pockets daily. They've been serving northeastern Pennsylvania for three generations. They guarantee their products and use only 100 percent natural ingredients. It's the kind of food quality that allows them to boast that they are the only "All-Natural Pennsylvania Pierogie." Lucky for you there are two locations, one in Jessup and one in Peckville.

Lancaster

Country Lane Furniture, FURNITURE, 1200 East Main St. (Rte. 422), Annville 17003; (717) 867-5701; clfstore.com. Hours: Mon and Wed 9 a.m. to 5 p.m.; Tues, Thurs, Fri 9 a.m. to 8 p.m.; Sat 8 a.m. to 4 p.m. It's hard to not find a furniture store in this part of Pennsylvania. Country Lane is one of the newer shops, opened in 1989. They use the same wood species as their ancestors. Their showroom is about 10,000 square feet of cherry, white oak, black walnut, elm, and maple furniture. All those woods are native to Pennsylvania. In fact, Lancaster County is home to the oldest English elm in the country (estimated at over 200 years old). Although they utilize the skills of Amish and Mennonite furniture makers, who specialize in primitive and Shaker furniture, you will see modern pieces, like microwave cabinets and TV stands. They do offer a selection of cottage, French country, and Mission- and Craftsman-styled pieces. Some of their furniture is inspired by these styles but designed for practical use. And not everything is covered with a hard wood finish, they offer cushioned sofas, gliders, and crib sets. You'll even see some wooden toys in the showroom or on their online catalog. It's true, Amish and Mennonite children do play—after the chores are done, of course.

The Extinctions Store, FOSSILS, 1809 Columbia Ave., Lancaster 17603; (717) 123-1234; extinctionsstore.com. Open Mon through Fri, 9 a.m. to 5 p.m. Steve Hess has been collecting fossils for 40 years. He supplies museums and collectors with his finds—and yes, he does his own fieldwork. If you think you've found a fossil but don't want to ruin it by cleaning it or chipping away "extra" dirt, Steve can advise you on your next step or do it for you. Even though he has been to excavation sites in Greece and Italy to discover ancient treasures, he loves his Pennsylvania fossils. While the state isn't filled with gems and gold, it is filled with sea fossils. Ancient plants, corals, shellfish, and trilobites, which look like giant pill bugs, are found in shale deposits that slice through the state's mountain ranges.

Fisher's Handmade Quilts, Crafts, & Fabrics, QUILTING/FABRICS, 2713 Old Philadelphia Pike, Bird in Hand 17505; (717) 392-5440. Open Mon through Sat, 9 a.m. to 5 p.m. Don't expect to connect with quilters in Amish country via texting or email. Their unique way of life closely resembles the way it was—simple and non-materialistic, with horse-powered vehicles and a slow daily pace. They live separated from the rest of the world to maintain this lifestyle. They weren't always so shy. One of the teachings of the Amish faith is called *the ban* or *shunning*. This is based on the interpretation of the New Testament's advice not to associate with a church member who does not repent of his sinful conduct. The purpose of this discipline is to help the member realize the error of his ways and to encourage his repentance, after which he would be restored to church fellowship. This excommunication was at first only applied at the communion table. However, the followers of Jacob Amman felt the unrepentant individual should be completely shunned or avoided by all church members. This belief, along with other differences, led to Amman's split with the Mennonites in 1693. His followers were later called Amish. They eagerly accepted William Penn's offer of religious freedom as part of Penn's "holy experiment" of religious tolerance. The first sizable group of Amish arrived in Lancaster County in the 1720s or 1730s. The quilts for which they are famous didn't truly evolve into an art form until the 1800s when their communities were better established. Patterns that you'll see often include LeMoyne Star, Pinwheel, Dutchman's Puzzle, Flock of Geese, and Churn Dash.

Flying Fibers, KNITTING, 329C Main St., Landisville 17538; (717) 898-8020; flyingfibers.com. Open Mon through Fri, 10 a.m. to 5 p.m.; Sat, 10 a.m. to 3 p.m. Also open until 8 p.m. on the 2nd and 4th Wed of each month. Flying Fibers is the mother-daughter team of Jeri Robinson-Lawrence and Irina Lawrence. Both women are passionate about providing beautiful products to crafters of any skill, as well as promoting the preservation of rare breed sheep. In addition to owning the shop, Jeri and Irina have a flock of rare breed Wensleydale sheep and endangered Leicester Longwool sheep. Based on the season, this local fiber is available in-store. Jeri's best friend, Ellen Anderson, is manager of Flying Fibers, so you'll see her in the shop throughout the week. These three women are extremely passionate about the fiber arts and are regularly willing to share their knowledge and expertise. They want to be your local source for all of your knitting, crochet, spinning, weaving, and felting needs. Flying Fibers specializes in yarn, fiber, and roving from rare breed and locally raised sheep as well as from other fiber-producing animals. They have a serious selection of sustainable, fair trade, and unusual fibers, yarns, and handmade products. It's their goal to provide the handspinner and felter with the largest selection of roving. Additionally, they are the exclusive US retailer for Wensleydale Longwool Sheep Shop Yarns. Other yarns in stock include Rowan, Baah, Classic Elite, Cascade, Universal, Zealana, Appalachian Baby Design, Skacel Yarns, The Alpaca Yarn Company, Frog Tree, Kraemer Yarns (of Nazareth, Pennsylvania), and more. Spinning and weaving equipment and supplies are available and in stock, including products from Ashford, Kromski, Louet, Schacht, and Majacraft.

Foltz Pottery, CERAMICS/POTTERY, 225 N. Peartown Rd., Reinholds 17569; (717) 336-2676; foltzpottery.com. Check the website for a list of hours. Ned Foltz grew up in Lancaster County, but graduated from the Philadelphia College of Art with a degree in graphic art. At 21 he began teaching art at Schuylkill Valley High

School. He taught himself to make German redware pottery during this time. After 18 years of teaching, he decided to make pottery his full-time career. In the first years, he dug his own clay and made tiles and small pieces that were sold at the Ephrata Cloister shop (Ephrata is about eight miles from Ned's shop). Over the years, his style changed and developed along with his business. He now creates pottery in several different ways. Some pieces are formed over molds, some are cast, and many are hand-turned and sculpted. His decorating styles have also expanded to include slip decorating, slip trail, cutwork, applied work, *sgrafitto* (a technique that involves scruffing or scratching through a surface to reveal a lower layer of a contrasting color), sponging, and stenciling. All Foltz pottery is made using 200-year-old Pennsylvania German traditional methods except for the glaze, which is lead-free and can be safely used with food. Ned now does between 20 and 30 shows a year, including some at his own shop and others at museums and craft shows in other states.

Forest Hill Leather Craft, LEATHER, 225 Forest Hill Rd., Bird-in-Hand, 17505; (717) 656-8758. Open Mon through Fri, 8 a.m. to 5 p.m. Forest Hill Leather Craft has been making belts, totes, bridles, saddles, and tack for more than 14 years. Located on an Amish farm, the owner Isaac Stolzfus works with quality leathers to satisfy the equestrian needs for all types of horse lovers. His shop is on premise, and you can see all of his hides in the shop online. He also makes wallets, purses, and saddle bags that are clean and simple. The leather products are made in the Amish style, unembellished and classic-looking. Isaac uses solid brass catches and hooks for the metalwork. The totes, portfolios, and attachés are almost Coach inspired. The leather is thick and sturdy without being too heavy. But you can almost feel its durability. In the Amish style, which is plain but not bland, you won't see overpowering colors, wacky designs, or strange combinations of straps. Isaac's work is practical and sensible, and will last for a long, long time.

Hanway Mill House, DECORATIVE BOXES, 763 Bellvue Ave., Gap 17527; (484) 753-3075; hanwaymillhouse.wordpress.com. Call ahead for studio hours. When you think of paper mache, you probably think of art class, cornstarch-sticky

fingers, and really bad results. But Barb Kauffman doesn't have any problems with stickiness or results. She uses this nontraditional method to make crafts that you'd swear were clay. She stencils, paints, and finishes paper mache boxes to look like the Shaker kind (the ones that cost almost as much as college tuition). Barb knows, however, what it feels like to not have money. In fact, limited resources, sometimes a necessity for creativity, are how she got into the craft business in the first place. One day, her husband came home and said he had bought a 200-year-old home. Not exactly the roses and chocolates most wives dream of, but she and her husband restored it. By the time they moved in, she didn't have the money to fill it with antiques to decorate it properly. So, Barb bought a new tin bucket, distressed it, painted it, and stained it to look like an antique. Pleased with the results, she graduated to furniture, boxes, and more. She made so much that she started selling the surplus. She's still selling the "surplus" on Etsy. She has boxes in every "flavor"—holidays, animals, and, her favorite, silhouettes. She gets her artistic inspiration from Pennsylvania with its four seasons, animals, and history.

JC Rugs, RUGS, featured at PA Guild of Craftsmen Store, 335 N. Queen St., Lancaster 17603; jcrugs.com. If Judy Carter was a mountain climber, she'd be scaling Mt. Everest right now. She loves a challenge, the harder the better. Her "base camp" of rug hooking began in her great-grandmother's attic with an old mystery rug—no one knew who had done the hooking. She took a class to learn the craft and was, of course, hooked. Many years ago, when rugs were handmade and homemade, some rug hookers would use old burlap feed sacks and scraps of old clothing, others used yarn on a linen base. The rugs had seasonal uses—on the floor for the summer and sometimes on the bed in the winter for warmth. Today, Judy uses wool and for backing, a stiff rug warp. She dyes her own wool, but also uses texture wool (plaids and checked patterns). She'll use up to 100 different types of wool in one piece. Her rugs take anywhere from 50 to 100 hours to complete. In her recent book, *Hooking Animals*, Judy explains that large amounts of varied types of wool are necessary to capture the difference between scales or fur or feathers. She's a stickler for the eyes—she believes it's necessary for capturing the essence of the subject. It's important for her to have a connection to the animal rather than the flat style that you may find with other mass-produced rugs. She also teaches workshops for attendees to learn to hook rugs that are the image of their pets.

Kunzler & Company, MEATS, 652 Manor St., Lancaster 17604; (888) 586-9537; kunzler.com. Open Mon through Fri, 8 a.m. to 4 p.m. In 1901 Christian F. Kunzler, a German immigrant, informed his widowed mother that he wanted to switch careers and become a butcher. She approved and that was that. He invested his life savings of $700 and began making sausage in Lancaster. From the very beginning Christian knew his very particular clientele well. His fellow German immigrants would only purchase meats from a trusted and traditional butcher. So, he insisted on using only the finest quality ingredients and the most rigorous methods to make his meat products. The Kunzler brand name is now recognized as one of the most respected in the industry. From hams, franks (aka hot dogs), bacon, luncheon meats, and specialty items such as Lebanon bologna (sweet and regular), Kunzler's manufactures over 500 quality meat products. Kunzler's products can be found in supermarkets, delicatessens, convenience stores, schools, theme parks, sports complexes, and finer restaurants throughout the US. As Kunzler & Company celebrates over 100 years of making meat products, they maintain their dedication to the Old World traditions of curing and smoking along with the recipes carried to the New World by Christian F. Kunzler.

Lapp's Toys & Furniture, FURNITURE/TOYS, 2220 Horseshoe Rd., Lancaster, 17572; (717) 768-7243; lappstoysandfurniture.com. Open Mon through Fri, 8 a.m. to 4 p.m. For more than 25 years the Lapp family has been producing wooden toys, doll furniture, children's furniture, toy chests, and distressed trunks and furniture. Hand-made and built to last, you can expect the very best. They are a family business and take pride in delivering the best wooden items to their wholesale and retail customers. They have over 100 different types of toys and toy boxes for kids of all ages. This includes cars, trucks, dolls, and doll furniture. They also carry wooden furniture for children and adults in the Amish and Shaker primitive styles. They recently moved their shop from Ronks and now have an additional 15,000 square feet of space to display their wares. Brothers John and Amos Lapp also have more woodworking space in which to make their puzzle boxes or trick boxes that can only be opened by a series of manipulations—a pull, push, or gentle squeeze. They make great holders for all your treasures.

Log Cabin Quilt Shop, QUILTING, 2679 Old Philadelphia Pike, Bird-In-Hand 17505; (717) 393-1702; lcquiltshop.com. Open Mon through Thurs and Sat, 9 a.m. to 5 p.m.; Fri, 9 a.m. to 6 p.m. A gem of a quilt shop in Amish country where you find quilts, quilted wall hangings, and *quillows* (quilt pillows) on display as well as the patterns, fabric, notions, and supplies needed to make them.

What's with all the weird names in Lancaster? In the early 1730s communication between German immigrants and English inhabitants was difficult, so pictorial signs became recognizable and understandable landmarks for travelers. When Old Philadelphia Pike (Route 340) was being laid out in order to create a direct route between Lancaster and Philadelphia, signs were an easy reference for the two cultures. At one point, a discussion took place between two road surveyors as to whether they should stop at their present location or go on to Lancaster to spend the night. One of them said, "A bird in the hand is worth two in the bush." And both remained at what became known as the Bird-in-Hand Inn. The sign in front of the inn portrayed a man with a bird in his hand and a bush nearby in which two birds were perched.

The Old Candle Barn, CANDLES, 3551 Old Philadelphia Pike, Intercourse 17534; (717) 768-8926; oldcandlebarn.com. Open Mon through Sat, 8 a.m. to 5 p.m. Self-guided tours of this candle-making factory are available, but be sure to call first, as the hours vary. John and Fannie Beiler began making candles in the basement of their home back in the late 1960s. Their candle-making business grew so rapidly that they moved the candle facility three times before settling in Intercourse. That was 1982, when the initial building was only 12,000 square feet. Today the building size has grown to approximately 28,000 square feet. The Beilers have since passed away and the Old Candle Barn is now owned and operated by the Hurst family. Local craftsmen hand dip candles using the old-fashioned method where long wicks are draped over a long hangar or pole and repeatedly dipped into melted wax and dried. Layer after layer hardens until the candle reaches the appropriate diameter. These quality handmade candles, including their line of primitive jars, ceramic crocks, and lumpy (also known as grubby) pillar candles are all sold in the gift shop.

If you're wondering how Intercourse got its name, one explanation centers around an old race track that existed along the Old Philadelphia Pike. The exit to the entrance of the race course was known as, "Enter course." It's believed that "Enter course" gradually evolved into "Intercourse." It still makes school kids giggle.

Peaceful Valley Amish Furniture, FURNITURE, 421 Hartman Bridge Rd. (Rt. 896), Strasburg 17579; (717) 687-8336; peacefulvalleyfurniture.com. Open Mon through Thurs, 9 a.m. to 5:30 p.m.; Fri, 9 a.m. to 7 p.m.; and Sat, 9 a.m. to 6 p.m. There are three locations throughout the county for the Peaceful Valley Amish handmade wood furniture. At each location, they have a large selection of fine furniture handcrafted by Amish and Mennonite artisans. But the Hartman Bridge location is the largest. They offer a wide variety of desks, cabinets, chests, tables, chairs (including the popular glider rockers), and more. They make baby cradles, doll cradles, benches, and birdhouses. They also make end tables—perfect for your bedside. Much of what you see will be crafted from hard woods such as oak, maple, and red cedar—all native to Pennsylvania. The choice of location for their main shop is ideal—lots of traffic passes by. In fact, the town of Strasburg was originally established as a stopping point along the Great Conestoga Road, which later became known as Strasburg Road. It's now famous for its railroads and train rides. Strasburg likes to boast that it was among the top ten most beautiful towns in Pennsylvania, as rated by The Culture Trip in 2015.

RGM, JEWELRY, 801 West Main St., Mount Joy 17552; (717) 653-9799; rgmwatches.com. Open by appointment only Mon through Fri, 9 a.m. to 5 p.m. RGM's commitment to excellence in watch design is apparent across their whole range—from their basic three-hand models to their epic tourbillons. Most cases and components are manufactured in the US and are hand-assembled. RGM just announced their third entirely in-house movement, Caliber 20, to celebrate their first 20 years of American watchmaking. Roland Murphy has five watchmakers working in the converted 1916 bank. They make mechanical watches that have to be wound daily, which is only 10 percent of the international watch market (quartz and battery-operated models make up the rest). Watches with handmade movements, the intricate network of balance springs and wheels that make mechanical watches tick, most often originate from countries such as China and Switzerland. While American companies such as Tiffany and Timex still exist, RGM is the last to make its own movements, producing 200 to 300 handmade watches a year, which sell for anywhere from $1,850 to $100,000 (for the gold-plated Pennsylvania Tourbillon, which has more than 200 parts, including a miniature cage that aims to counter the effects of gravity). These are ornately crafted, minimally designed watches, renowned for their quality and uniqueness.

Ridge Hollow Game Boards, TOYS/GAME BOARDS, 14 Ridge Dr., Lititz 17543; (717) 626-1395; ridgehollow@gmail.com; ridgehollowgameboards.com. Barbara Wagaman takes play seriously. She designs and creates wooden game boards that are decorative and functional. Barb grew up in an 1876 Colonial farmhouse with her family. She earned a degree in fine arts/design and has an eye for the Colonial-era painting style. Her painting is greatly influenced by her Pennsylvania German heritage. Barb credits her mother Marion, a talented folk artist, for instilling in her a deep appreciation and love of early America. Her childhood activities also contributed to her future career. As a child, board games were a large part of country living—family and friends spending time together, long summer afternoons with cousins playing Parcheesi and Chinese Checkers. In 1986 Barb painted a Parcheesi game on an old bread board as a birthday gift to her husband Phil. The gift inadvertently began a 28-year adventure in the making of wooden game boards. Her rustic Colonial representations of the well-known games look as if she stole Ben Franklin's very own checkerboard. Her Ship Parcheesi gameboard has a nautical theme, with miniature lighthouses and compass roses.

Stoudt's Brewery, BREWERY, 2800 North Reading Rd., Adamstown 19501; (717) 484-4386; stoudts.com. Tours offered Sat, 3 p.m. and Sun, 1 p.m. Restaurant hours are Mon through Thurs, 4 to 9 p.m.; Fri and Sat, noon to 10 p.m.; Sun, 11:30 a.m. to 8 p.m. Stoudt's claim to fame is that they are Pennsylvania's first microbrewery. Pioneer of the craft beer movement, Ed Stoudt is an old-school beer geek and his passion is evident in the beers. In 1987, Ed's wife Carol Stoudt became the first woman to open a brewery since Prohibition. She is known in the industry as the "Queen of Hops." In fact some may say that the women who have since entered the manly art of brewing beer owe a bit of thanks to Carol who has pushed the "glass" ceiling. But in truth both Ed and Carol are well liked and respected for their quality beer. The brewery, headed by this devoted and unforgettable couple, offers a variety of authentic lagers and ales. You can also enjoy the cozy atmosphere of their brew pub restaurant where you can sample over 12 different styles of handcrafted beer and a full menu, which includes entrees prepared in beer and ales.

Thistle Finch Distillery, **DISTILLERY, 417 W. Grant St., Lancaster 17603; (717) 478-8472; thistlefinch.com. Open Wed through Thurs, 6 p.m. to 10 p.m.; Fri, 6 to 11 p.m.; and Sun, 2 to 8 p.m. Free distillery tours offered Sat, 3 p.m.** Built in the 1900s, the building that houses the Thistle Finch (or *distlefink* in Pennsylvania Dutch) Distillery began life as the Walter Schnader tobacco warehouse and is now listed on the National Registry of Historical Buildings. The distillery uses traditional methods (why mess with a good thing?) updated with a bit of modern knowledge to create an un-aged whiskey. Their award-winning Rye (60 percent rye, 30 percent wheat, and 10 percent malted barley) is made with locally grown grains. Unlike their beer brewing (there's a brewery on site too), Thistle Finch Distillery does not separate the solids from the liquid before fermenting their whiskey. They believe that distilling "on the grain" gives the end product more flavor. It may seem unusual for an establishment that makes and sells alcohol to be located in the heart of the strict Amish country, but the Amish do imbibe moderately and have always made their own alcoholic beverages. So, Thistle Finch Distillery fits right in.

Turkey Hill Dairy, **DAIRY, 2601 River Rd., Conestoga 17516; (800) 693-2479; turkeyhill.com.** Over 80 years ago, Armour Frey delivered milk. Bottles rattled in the back of his horse-drawn cart before the sleepy sun came up. Customers welcomed his daily delivery. Not the choicest of jobs, but it was the Great Depression and every penny helped. Slowly, as America recovered, Armour's route grew. Loyal customers requested more milk and other dairy products. The Freys needed more cows and more suppliers—so they reached out to the community of dairymen. And their business kept growing. Today they sell milk and ice cream to people in 38 states. One of Turkey Hill's partners is Brubaker Farms in Mount Joy. Brubaker was recognized as the most innovative farm in the nation in 2011. Brothers Mike and Tony Brubaker are raising their families side by side to maintain that reputation. No-till planting has become more than a recent growing trend in farming—it's the only method used at Brubaker Farms. That means that old crop remnants are left in the fields, while a special tiller plants new seeds throughout the rich organic matter of decayed old roots. This technique prevents erosion. Turkey Hill has also branched out beyond dairy to include a franchise of convenience gas stations and mini-markets dotted throughout the area, all of which carry (surprise!) Turkey Hill ice cream.

Lawrence

Apple Castle, FARM, 277 Route 18, New Wilmington 16142; (724) 652-3221; applecastle.com. Open daily, Aug to Nov, 9 a.m. to 8 p.m.; Dec through July, 9 a.m. to 5:30 p.m. An apple orchard that's 150 years old should know a few things about apples. They admit, though, that they are still improving and adding new varieties. Pennsylvanians love their apples. Each year the state harvests nearly 100 different varieties. In the past, nearly every Pennsylvania farm had a small orchard of apple trees, which yielded apples from July to November. Apples were essential to the survival of the farmers and were eaten at every meal for most of the year. Harvesting and preparing the apples was labor intensive; farmers and their families worked together to make cider, dried apples, vinegar, applesauce, and apple butter. Apple butter, a non-dairy apple preserve, is attributed to the Pennsylvania German settlers dating back to the mid-1700s. Before they could rely on refrigeration, the local farmers had to sugar cure then smoke their meat, pickle the vegetables, and dry the fruit. They noted that applesauce became rancid before the end of winter. They found that with a longer cooking process of the apples and cider, they could produce a tasty condiment that could get them through the winter. It may be called Apple Castle, but this place also grows and harvests peaches, nectarines, and blueberries, as well as sweet corn. They also produce their own honey—which is perfect on top of their apples.

Lebanon

Pennsylvania Soy Candles, CANDLES, 150 Rocherty Rd., Lebanon 17042; (717) 565-9667; pasoy.com. Heavenly scents invade the workplace of Richard and Carolyn Albright. Imagine inhaling calming or invigorating and spicy fragrances all day long. It's not as celestial as it sounds. The Albrights work hard blending scents, pouring and testing candles, managing sales and supply, and travelling frequently to almost 30 craft shows each year. They do their best to keep in touch with clients even while on the road. One of the couple's biggest pleasures is to provide scripture-based messages on their candles. In a state that has religious roots, candles that inspire come naturally. So, Carolyn says, not only does the scent lift your spirits, the enjoyer of the scents receives Biblical encouragement as well. Carolyn started as simply loving candles. She always collected and burned her favorite candle scents. Richard challenged her one day to start making her own. Her response: Who would buy them? She and Richard now have hundreds of fans, buyers, and inspired clients who love their scents and the fact that the candles, including the soy material, are made in Pennsylvania. A list of retail shops in which you can find their products is available online.

Seltzer's Smokehouse Meats, MEAT, 230 College St., Palmyra, 17078; (717) 838-6336; seltzerslebanon.com. Hours: Mon to Fri 8 a.m. to 5 p.m. Before the age of refrigeration and preservatives, German immigrants incorporated Old World butchering, fermenting, and curing techniques to keep meat safe and edible (and delicious). In 1902, Harvey Seltzer, a Pennsylvania-born butcher, created an ideal blend of beef and unique spices for his Lebanon bologna. This bologna became so popular that he went on to produce it commercially. This Pennsylvania Dutchman named his company after the town in which he lived, Palmyra Bologna Company. He refused to become totally modernized and remove the taste from the meat. You'll still see tall wooden smokehouses on the property. Bologna aficionados will tell you that the smoked meat flavor is what makes this party tray favorite so delicious. You can eat it sliced in a sandwich too—make sure you specify regular or sweet when ordering. The sweet bologna has sugar and spices added. A while back, when the federal government began inspecting meatpacking plants, Seltzer's had the honor of being the first federally inspected Lebanon bologna company. Today it's one of the oldest continually USDA-inspected operations. The bologna is available in the deli, at supermarkets, or online—a modern option with which Harvey Seltzer would probably be okay.

Lehigh

Braided Love, JEWELRY, 1259 Cedar Crest, Allentown 18103; (610) 737-1204; braidedlovebywendaboyer.com. Open studio, call ahead for hours. Wenda Boyer uses an unusual, but very versatile, medium—horsehair. The hair from the tail or mane of a horse has been used for commercial purposes for centuries. Horsehair plaster was widely used by builders to shore up walls. Horsehair was also used as a stuffing or batting for sofas and chairs. Anyone who has renovated an old home or reupholstered an antique chaise knows how long-lasting and tough equine hair can be. Wenda appreciates the strength of the creature and its hair. She takes the collected, combed, and cleaned hair and braids or weaves it into earrings, bracelets, and necklaces. Once braided, horsehair achieves an almost stiff, wiry feel, but it's also flexible. She is also able to knot the hair into intricate designs and add charms and clasps just as any jeweler would. Admittedly, first-time customers are

There's No People
Like Show People

Below is an additional list of Pennsylvania crafters that sell their wares at area craft shows around the state.

All Strings Considered, 6848 Mount Davis Rd., Meyersdale 15552. Birgitta Nostring spins her own hand-dyed yarn and creates one-of-a-kind, customized, handwoven rugs in the village of Summit Mills. She considers herself a traditional rag rug weaver. Her son Hans is more the "fluffy" weaver—he allows for an afghan fringe selvage. He's also the goat keeper. That means from animal (wool and mohair) to spun skein of yarn, they've had their hands in it.

Dog House Quilts, P.O. Box 973, Meadville 16335; (814) 977-1912; doghousequilts.com. Combining her love of sewing and quilting with her love of dogs is the perfect match for artisan Gerry Deane. Dog House Quilts was started in the summer of 2007 with an array doggie-inspired quilts, table runners, aprons, guest towels, agility bags, wall hangings, pillowcases, and sheets. Gerry also customizes the quilts to be breed-specific. And if your best friend is a loveable mutt from the shelter, she does non-breed specific specialty items, too.

Dragonfly's Lair, Ridgeway 15853; (814) 773-7660; etsy.com/shop/dragonflyslair. Lori Elias designs, crafts, and creates jewelry with metal and semiprecious gemstones. She primarily uses copper, but is starting to use a little silver and makes her own components in her studio. She hammers texture in copper and then lets it oxidize. She also works in polymer clay. She's self-taught in those media. For her clients, Lori includes a card that will give them the folklore behind each gem or stone. She shares a bit of the history or some of the attributes of the particular stone. She also uses pieces of Pennsylvania. Lori uses pebbles or feathers she collects on walks or travels throughout her area, called "found art," as a way of putting Pennsylvania in her work.

Ivy League Lip Balm, State College 15814; etsy.com/shop/IvyLeague LipBalm. Susannah Poese raises the bees that make the beeswax that provides the base for the lip balm she makes that will help fund her college tuition. She's one of the youngest Pennsylvania entrepreneurs. At age nine she created lip balms, designed labels for the tubes, and sold her products on Etsy. And she sells them at Penn State football home games. Her lip flavors include: "The Search for Spearmint," "Orange Ya Glad," "Fizzy Pop," and "Want S'more?" Her ingredients are all natural.

Kratz Eirer (Scratch eggs), Jim Thorpe 18229; etsy/thedistelfinktree.com. Decorating and dyeing eggs is a tradition that dates to the ancient Egyptians. Coleen I. McCauley carries on the tradition. It began at her grandmother's house with her grandmother's egg tree, a tradition carried over from Germany. Coleen uses natural dyes made from onion skins and vinegar to dye her eggs and a needle (early scratchers used sewing needles, pocket knives, or awls).

Lilith's Apothecary, Philadelphia 19134; lilithsapothecary@gmail.com; etsy.com/shop/lilithsapothecary. Sarah Powell, herbalist and a bit of a magician, handcrafts natural skin care products. From facials to lip balms, she adds expertise and a hint of her own TLC.

Miller's Homemade Soaps, Westfield; millershomemadesoaps.com. Barb Miller was a big fan of the concept of homesteading, not all of it, mind you. It's a tough life. But she was attracted to the idea of handmade soap; it fit well with the back to the land aspect of homesteading. When she and her husband moved to their Westfield farm in 1999, she began to sell vegetables at the farmers' market. Pennsylvania's growing season is short, so Barb made and sold soaps to supplement her income in the off season. She offers a variety of scents.

The Pennsylvania Broom Closet, 55 Tennessee Gas Rd., Troy 16947; thepabroomcloset.com. This broom company uses a 1890s broom-making apparatus and presents about nine broom-making demonstrations annually.

Peach Bottom Slate Co., Delta 17314. Rebecca Colby and husband James love their mallets, the ones they use for hand crafting ornamental and functional slate products. Featured as a finalist on Martha Stewart American Made Awards, the couple favor mallets over accolades and slate over any other medium you can name.

Rebecca Francis Rag Rugs, Dillsburg 17019. While Rebecca Francis specializes in hand woven rag rugs, she's actually weaving two parts of the state's history together: the more eco-friendly current trends with the thrifty, use-whatever-you-have-handy method of weaving from decades gone by. She uses an 18th-century loom, which lowers her carbon footprint while keeping the tradition alive. And she uses natural materials (hemp, wool, cotton) as well as recycled clothes.

RoseBlu Beads, Quakertown 18951; etsy.com/shop/RoseBluBeads. Patti Parker began bead weaving as a teenager. She has always loved beads, and taught herself the basic stitches and went from there. She shops at local bead stores when possible, and has been collecting beads for years. She'll also go to specialty beads shows, auctions, and flea markets to find local beads.

Slate Accents, 230 Palmer Dr., Clarion 16214; (814) 764-5516; slateaccents.com. When Brad Coulson was driving home from work one day and saw a slate roof being thrown in a dumpster, he stopped and asked

a bit squeamish when the material of her pieces' origin is revealed. But if you're a horse lover and have groomed a horse, there's an unabashed admiration for taking such a mundane "yarn" and knitting it into something that will last longer than your great-grandma's chairs. Wenda also creates customized pieces for any horse owner who wishes to keep their dear friend close to his or her heart.

The Conestoga Company, TOYS AND GAMES, 323 Sumner Ave., Allentown 18102; (800) 987-BANG; bigbangcannons.com. Open Mon through Fri, 8 a.m. to 4:30 p.m. Once the international hub of steel and iron, Allentown has downsized its metal output considerably. But Conestoga still makes cannons—toy cannons. In 1907 a professor of physics at Lehigh University patented a "gas gun" that was hailed as a safe alternative to fireworks. The Big-Bang Cannon was a sensation among adults and children. The miniature cannon uses a special ammunition call "Bangsite," which is pulverized calcium carbide. That mixture, plus air, water, and a spark makes a pleasing bang. While the cannon (no longer than a computer keyboard) is safe (read: no gunpowder), the company recommends adult supervision for kids under the age of 16 and for all users to employ the same sort of common sense as you would when using any toy that has a barrel. Keep your face away from the business end, don't aim it at your sibling (no matter how angry you are with him or her), and be mindful of bystanders and pets. The company also has an online decibel comparison chart so you see how noises stack up. Note: Rock music is louder than some of their cannons. Originally called the Gas Cannon Company, the name was changed to the Toy Cannon Works in 1916. They made and sold Breech Loading Cannons. In 1924, the name was changed again to Conestoga Cannon Company. If cannons aren't your thing, the company also has brass planes, boats, and tanks.

Conversational Threads Fiber Arts Studio, KNITTING, 6 South 4th St., Emmaus 18049; (610) 421-8889; conversationalthreads.com. Open Mon, Thurs, and Fri, noon to 7 p.m.; Tues and Wed, 11 a.m. to 5 p.m.; Sat, 11 a.m. to 5 p.m.; and Sun, 1 to 5 p.m. If you knit or crochet, walking through the door of this establishment is like walking into to the Land of Oz. There are needles, notions, and a rainbow of yarn in every thickness imaginable, all sorts of fibers, and accessories—ones you never even knew existed. Some wools are spun so soft and fluffy, you may spend the first 15 minutes of your visit just petting the displays. Suppliers of wool, yarn, and organic fibers homegrown and imported were once deemed something "only granny needs." But stalkers of Pinterest and DIYers everywhere know the value of handmade accessories—and appreciate the labor that goes into them. Even something as simple as a hand-knitted scarf is worth more than a similar one purchased at a mega-market. Less stress on the environment, relaxing work with your hands, and the sentimental value are priceless. Fiber arts also tie you to your neighbors. In 2011, when owner Cindy Fitzpatrick was fighting breast cancer and subsequent leukemia, she almost closed the business. But her patrons came to the rescue and kept her studio running—at no charge. Fitzpatrick's Conversational Threads has knitted together a community of devoted fiber friends.

Funk Brewing Company, BREWERY, 19 S. 6th St., Emmaus 18049; (610) 421-8270; funkbrewing.com. Open Thurs, 5 to 10 p.m.; Fri, 4 to 10 p.m.; Sat, noon to 10 p.m.; and Sun, noon to 7 p.m. Kyle Joseph Funk, Joe to his fans, owns a microbrewery that locals love. IPAs, Double IPAs, and Porters—they love them all. Fair warning, though, don't get in front of his fans in February when the Lehigh Valley hosts its annual Beer Week, as they're likely to run you over for a pint of Funk brew. In 2013, Pennsylvania ranked sixth in the Top Ten List of Craft Beers and/or Microbreweries in the US according to *USA Today*. At that point the state had 93 (more than Wisconsin!) microbreweries. Pre-Prohibition Pennsylvania had six well-developed, commercial breweries—more than any other state in the 1920s. In 2014 Funk Brewing Company made history by being the first brewpub permitted in the village of Emmaus. The village was originally settled in 1740s by Moravian (a Reformed Lutheran sect from Germany) immigrants who also settled in the towns of Bethlehem and Nazareth. They brought their love of beer and brewing with them and passed it down to their descendants. Joe and his Funk Brewing Company are members of the Brewers Association, so you know he's serious. This is no side job. His motto? Pushing the Limits of Craft Beer.

Josh Early Candies, CANDY/CHOCOLATE, 4640 Tilghman St., Allentown 18104; (610) 395-4321; joshearlycandies.com. **Open Mon through Sat, 9 a.m. to 9 p.m.; Sun, noon to 6 p.m.** In the early 1900s, Joshua Mark Early III and a partner sold wholesale candy under the company name of Richardson and Early. The love of chocolate was passed along to his son, Josh Early IV who, along with his wife Millie, started their own retail business in Reading. They called the store Early's Old Fashioned Chocolates. In 1938 they offered the city their first batch of buttercreams. Their son, Josh Early V, took an interest in confections and the family worked together over the years developing recipes for delicious chocolates for lucky locals. They perfected their philosophy of putting quality first and worked on their recipes. In 1956 Josh V began making and selling candy wholesale in nearby Baumstown. He and his wife Marge worked there for five years before opening their own retail store in Allentown. The new business thrived. Their candy line expanded—chocolates, buttercreams, hard candies, and chocolate-covered fruits and nuts. And their staff expanded, Josh and Marge's son-in-law, Barry Dobil, joined them in 1972. These modern master candymakers continue to use the same recipes developed in the early 1900s. Sweetness runs in their DNA, because four other family members continue the tradition of Josh Early Candies, and they are now a fifth-generation family business. Hint: It's a crowded store during the holidays, so you might want to order online or arrive early (no pun intended).

Linda Gettings Beadwork, BEADWORK, Center Valley 18034; (610) 797-7537. **Studio hours by appointment only.** Linda has been designing and teaching bead weaving and wirework for more than 20 years. She has had over 100 of her designs published in many of the major beading magazines. She worked for many years organizing and teaching classes for Innovative Bead Expo and continues to teach classes at local bead stores and for bead societies. Her love of beads started when she was a little girl, and her mother gifted her with her first set of pop-beads. Over the years school, marriage, children, and life got in the way. When her youngest child was born, she moved from the publishing business to get a part-time job, spending about two days a week at a bead store. She was like a kid in a

candy shop and discovered her talent for creating her own designs. She loves all the Native American beading pieces in Pennsylvania as well as all around the country. She's also been inspired by Pennsylvania's natural beauty and its residential neighborhoods. In one of her early articles in *Beadwork* magazine, she shares how she was sitting at a stoplight looking at a home with a white picket fence covered in an amazing array of flowers. It inspired her white picket fences pattern for her cuffs and bracelets. Her book, *Great Beaded Gifts*, has been released in hard and soft cover and is available on Amazon.com.

Penn Big Bed Slate Co. Inc., SLATE, 8450 Brown St., Slatington 18080; (610) 767-4601; pennbigbedslate.com. Open Mon through Thurs, 10 a.m. to 7 p.m. Headquartered in Slatington, this company has mined and manufactured slate products since 1934. Penn Big Bed Slate Company (PBBS) has been a family owned enterprise since its founding by Jacob Papay and his four sons John, Tom, Mike, Steve, and son-in-law Steve Babyak. Today Pete Papay Sr. and his son Pete Papay Jr. are the third- and fourth-generation quarriers. Their products are used in roofing, construction, and architectural applications such as windowsills, countertops, mantles, lavatories, fireplaces, and floor tiles. They also make a wide variety of slate for turkey calls and craft slate. Slate has endured as one of the most desired products for architectural and custom design work. Its uniqueness as a building material lies in its inherent capacity to be sheared into flat sheets of nearly any size. PBBS is the leading supplier of Pennsylvania slate nationwide. Clear slate is one-color slate, which is all from one "bed" or formation. Ribbon slate is formed by Mother Nature when two or more formations are compressed to make one stone from more than two beds. The contrast looks like a ribbon embedded between lighter colored beds of stone.

Pinnacle Ridge Winery, WINERY, 407 Old Route 22, Kutztown 19530; (610) 756-4481; pinridge.com. Open seasonally Mon through Sun, 10 a.m. to 6 p.m. Call first to confirm hours. It was supposed to be a retirement business for owner Brad Knapp, something he could get into and then move away from as he became older. Somehow, it became an all-consuming passion. Brad dabbled a little in winemaking prior to his establishment of Pinnacle Ridge. And with a PhD in analytical chemistry, he sure knew the beauty of the resulting reaction of yeast added to crushed grapes. Brad bought the land, a strip of fields and hills along old Route 22, in 1990 and opened his winery to the public in 1995—with just three wines. He now offers over 20. The winery in Kutztown produces sparkling wines— one particularly fun bubbly is Pinnacle Ridge's Blanc de Blanc—as well as reds and whites. Brad's love of wines and his connection with the community have given him an opportunity to pursue his love of music. The Winery's bank barn (complete with Pennsylvania Dutch hexsigns on the front) hosts music events. Welcoming spring, the first music event starts in May and subsequent weekend jams run through the growing season. A separate musical event in October called Blues in the Barn celebrates the harvest.

Premise Maid Candies, CANDY/CHOCOLATE, 10860 Hamilton Blvd., Breinigsville 18031; (610) 395-3221; premisemaid.com. Open Mon through Sat, 9 a.m. to 9 p.m.; Sun, 11 a.m. to 6 p.m. Summer hours are Mon through Sat, 9 a.m. to 9:30 p.m.; Sun, 11 a.m. to 9:30 p.m. Premise Maid Candies is a chocolate village with a candy shop, bakery, and ice cream shop. It is a family-owned business that was the vision of William Damiano. Established in 1979, it was founded on the notion that all the chocolates had to be made on the premises. Thus, the company name. They began in a humble 700-square-foot store in Fleetwood, with a few family members and one employee. William defined the company's philosophy: Never sacrifice quality for convenience. William began selling wholesale to Hess's department stores (an old retail chain in eastern Pennsylvania) and other card and gift shops. In 1984 the buildings of an old farmstead became Premise Maid's present location. Their facility consists of a stone barn, carriage house, and farmhouse on a two-acre site in Breinigsville. All the structures date back to the pre–Civil War era and have been restored to retain their Old World charm. The Damiano family did most of the work themselves, hiring contractors only when needed. Since 1984 the buildings at Premise Maid have grown into a small village. The bakery and the chocolate shop are filled with an assortment of freshly baked desserts, hard candies, and the company's well-known chocolates. The three-story stone barn is home to their confectionery manufacturing and also houses the ice creamery, which serves 40 flavors of premium ice cream. William's son Joe became "Chief Candyman" of Premise Maid in 1986 and is assisted by approximately 50 employees. The second and third generations of the Damiano family are determined to continue the family tradition of manufacturing amazing chocolates, ice cream, and bakery items from family recipes.

Weaver Lure, SPORTING EQUIPMENT, 630 E. Green St., Allentown 18109; (610) 433-5980; weaverlure.com. Open Mon through Fri, 9 a.m. to 5 p.m. Weaver Lure's motto is "Made by fishermen for fisherman." They have been a Pennsylvania fishing lure manufacturer for over 45 years. In a small corner of the state that's practically on top of the Lehigh River, the Weaver Lure company lures many a fisherman (and woman). Their Weaver Grabber spoons and spinners, along with their Mini Latch bait threader and snelled treble hooks, have been a go-to lure on many East Coast streams and lakes. Snelled treble hooks, are curved, barbed hooks that are the most often used hooks in fishing. Not a fisherperson? Or can't make it Allentown today? That's okay, they demonstrate how to use all of their products online with clear illustrations. This includes the rather unnerving process of threading a live minnow on a spinner. It's cruel, but it works. Once on the wire lure, the minnow thrashes about madly, which in turn attracts the attention of hungry fish. And, bam! You're having fish for dinner.

Wilz Pottery, CERAMICS/POTTERY, P.O. Box 434, Macungie 18062; (215) 260-1133; wilzpottery.com. Note to self: To change your life's course drastically, take an adult night course on pottery. Computer programmer Denise Wilz had put in 20 years of bytes and characters. It was time for a change. After falling in love with pottery class, she got in touch with her Pennsylvania German roots and discovered the beauty of redware and an ancient technique called *sgraffito* (Italian for "scratching"). Redware is pottery formed from a type of ubiquitous clay that fires at low temps to a deep burnt orange finish. The color of the terra cotta clay is due to the iron oxide (think rust) it contains. When German settlers came to the newly purchased Penn's Woods, they had nothing and were living in lean-tos and caves. Everyday items such as plates, bowls, and cups were luxuries. Once they recognized that the clay found here was the same sort of clay plentiful in their home country, they formed rough shapes into functional pieces. As the colonies prospered, the desire for more decorative bowls and serving platters developed. Wilz specializes in redware using *sgraffito* to etch traditional line drawings of tulips and doves onto pottery. She also creates slipware pieces. Slip is pottery jargon for watery, light clay (may contain lead or manganese) mixed with water. The slip coats the top layer of redware with a yellowish film. Denise takes a wire tool and, tracing the line drawings, gently scratches away the slip to reveal the glorious burnt orange underneath. In much of the Pennsylvania German folk art, you'll see a bird that looks like a dove, called *distlefink*, German for "thistle finch," which is also known as the European gold finch. The bird represents happiness, peace, and friendship. Another recurring symbol is the tulip, or stylized lily. Lilies are symbolic of faith, hope, and purity. Denise's creations can be found at the Mennonite Heritage Center at 565 Yoder Road in Harleysville (212-256-3020; open Tues through Fri, 10 a.m. to 5:00 p.m.; Sat, 10 a.m. to 2 p.m.).

Yocco's Hot Dog King, HOT DOGS, 2128 Hamilton St., Allentown 18049; (610) 821-8488; yoccos.com. Open Mon through Fri, 9 a.m. to 5 p.m. Sometimes cultures collide. Other times they mesh into a successful business. Italian entrepreneur Theodore Iacocca (uncle of Lee Iacocca, Chrysler's famous CEO) opened a hot dog stand in Allentown in 1922. Its original name was Liberty Grill. All was good, the business expanded, and the name changed to Iacocca's. But the Pennsylvania Dutch patrons couldn't pronounce the name. On paper, it looked like *yah-cohz* to them. Out of deference to the local customers, the name was changed again to Yocco's. Gary Iacocca, the third-generation owner, refers to himself as the company's chief cook and bottle washer. He was working at the hotdog stand while attending graduate school. Not just for summer or the ballpark, Yocco's hot dogs are good any time of the year. In fact, they're better in the winter, especially with Yocco's secret recipe chili sauce. If you're not a hot dog fan, don't dispair; they offer cheesesteaks, French fries, and pierogies as well. The company has six locations (as of this printing) in the Lehigh Valley at which you can enjoy a crazy-yummy hot dog. And they sell a to-go "Pic-Nic Pac" that you can take to work and be the hero of your office (or home!).

Luzerne

Abby's Doggone Good Gourmet, PETS, P.O. Box 62, Dalmatia 17017; (800) 432-9443; info@dogsloveabbys.com; dogsloveabbys.com. Opened by Susan

Kaminski in 1993 and named after her dog, Abby's Doggone Good Gourmet offers doggie treats, snacks, and cookies that are a hit with the canine crowd. Susan is doing well these days with the people crowd, too. Her treats have won praise all across the country and have had positive reviews from magazines such as *Maxim* and *Good Dog!* Her products include cookies of all kinds with names like Turkey Pot Pie Cookies, Bacon n' Egg Barkers, Cheddar Cheese Munchkins, Swirly-Qs, and Boney ma Roneys. And since dogs and cats have difficulty processing chocolate (pets often consume it accidentally with fatal results), Susan has created Berry Good Carob Bears. These are bear-shaped cookies drizzled with melted vanilla yogurt and carob chips. Carob comes from the locust bean, related to the pea family of plants. It's important, she notes, to give dogs dog treats not people treats. Her website sells to wholesalers and retailers and directly to you.

Candelles, CANDLES, 9 E Broad St., Hazelton 18201; candelles.com. Open Mon through Fri, 7 a.m. to 3 p.m.; Sat, 8 to 2 p.m. It's hard to imagine that failure and cancer brought Kelley Major and CJ Graaf to their successful candle business. It started as just a hobby, something they'd learn together. But Kelley and CJ found themselves burning through their homemade candles in one day and spending too much money replacing them. They knew something was wrong; it was time to do some research. They learned the (huge) difference between paraffin and soy waxes. They tested their own soy wax and loved it. But the learning curve was much steeper than they anticipated. After opening a little online shop, they discovered their candlewicks were faulty and ended up refunding all their customers. They shut down, embarrassed, thinking they'd never pour candles again. Months later, when Kelley's grandmother was diagnosed with cancer, they wanted to do something to support and help with the medical bills. They bravely went back to pouring candles as a fundraiser, making her grandmother's favorite scents. Late-night talks brought Kelley and her grandmother closer than ever. Kelley's grandmother observed Kelley's passion and joy in developing the scents for the candles. "Work hard," she advised Kelley. "Follow your dreams, make life worth living." Kelley's grandmother passed away within a month of her diagnosis. Kelley and CJ needed to find happiness to bring them out of their grief. They gave candles another try. After more research and wick testing, they opened Candelles in November 2013. Clients and customers are happy with their candles, which are offered at Hallmark stores throughout the country. Memories of Kelley's grandmother shine through, a light to their (tested) wicks.

Duvall Leatherwork, LEATHER, 314 Wyoming Ave., Kingston 18704; (570) 283-9297; duvallleatherwork.com. Open Mon through Fri, 8 a.m. to 5 p.m.; Sat, 8 a.m. to 1 p.m. Nick Duvall is the kind of person who keeps his workstation neat. He likes careful, calm, and precise, which is exactly what you have to be when you work with leather—you don't get do-overs. One wrong cut and you obliterate hours of work in an instant. Most people would be frustrated by such an unforgiving medium, but ever since Nick was a kid he's been interested in leather. He apprenticed with an English saddler long enough to learn the jargon and techniques. In truth, he's "98 percent self-taught." Nick and his employees create a range of items, from serious historical reproduction gear (for Civil War reenactors) to wallets. Duvall Leatherwork is mixing it up with canvas and leather bags and belts. Nick's clients are people like him, who recognize and demand quality work along with a little bit of quirky (check out his leather carrying cases for growlers). They also want something durable, handmade, and homemade. Working with leather is a skill that nearly died out with the industrial age and later with the introduction of plastic materials that were often substituted for hide. Nick makes sure his leather hides are from US tanners, including one from Pennsylvania.

Lion Brewery, BREWERY, 350 Laird St., Wilkes-Barre 18702; (570) 823-8801; lionbrewery.com. Guided tours and tastings are available year round; call ahead to arrange. For over 110 years some serious suds have been coming out of the ferocious Stegmaier Brewing Company. Begun in 1905, it started its brewing journey as Luzerne County Brewing Company. It changed hands a few times, eventually becoming known as the Lion Brewery. The brewery managed to squeak through Prohibition like other breweries by making "near-beer," which has about 1 percent alcohol by volume (ABV). The Stegmaier brand was acquired from the Stegmaier Brewery, also located in Wilkes-Barre in 1974. Lionshead has been their flagship beer, but they also produce a root beer called Lion Brewery Root Beer, which contains no preservatives. Lion Brewery is the second largest brewery in the state, and overall they are the 15th largest American-owned brewery, selling over 750,000 cases annually.

Susquehanna Brewing Company, BREWERY, 635 S Main St., Pittston 18640; (570) 654-3557; sbcbeer.com. Open Mon through Fri, 9 a.m. to 5 p.m. In three years this brewing business received three awards for their beer. At the Annual Best of Craft Beer Awards, the president Ed Maiers served up his Pils-Noir and So-Wheat beers. A few days later, back at the office, he heard his son yelling about the two gold and one bronze medals the Susquehanna Brewing Company had won. So they celebrated, with beer, of course. The process of brewing beer is relatively simple and just about everything can go wrong. You start with four basic ingredients: grain (such as barley), hops with sugar (hops is a climbing plant that can grow just about anywhere), yeast, and water. The barley is soaked in hot water; the sugar is boiled with the hops. Once things cool down a bit, you mix all the ingredients together and add the yeast and the solution begins to ferment. In the process, the yeast releases alcohol. Well, the barley can go bad, the yeast can die, and the sugar can turn everything into a soppy mess. This is why you should let Ed do the cooking.

Lycoming

Crain Graphics, WOODWORKING, 241 Baxter Rd., Montoursville 17754; (570) 435-0646; libbycr25@verizon.net. With a name like Bob Crain, you'd think it would be inevitable that he paint and carve birds. Some artists are destined. Bob believes (a la Aristotle) that in all things of nature, there's something of the marvelous. He attempts to depict that "something" in all his work. He's a self-taught painter and bird wood carver. He bases his work on personal experience and the details of nature's many treasures. Lookout *Duck Dynasty*, Bob's wood carvings are more likely to attract waterfowl than a genuine duck call. He tries to portray the individual characteristics of each subject. He starts by drawing a pattern and cutting it from a block of basswood. He shapes the piece, like most woodoworkers, with knives and chisels, but then goes farther by texturing the piece with wood-burning pens. He finishes by painting the piece with acrylics. He does under-painting in gray tones and then adds a glaze to protect the color. Bob's work has appeared on and in magazines such as *Pennsylvania Game News* and *Fur-Fish-Game*.

Inspirations Quilt Shop, QUILTING, 701 Allegheny St., Jersey Shore 17740; (570) 398-7399; inspirationsquiltshop.net. Open Tues through Thurs, 11 a.m. to 4 p.m.; Fri, 11 a.m. to 5 p.m.; Sat, 11 a.m. to 3 p.m. In an old high school building, quilting is alive and well. The Inspirations Quilt Shop (IQS) promotes, supplies, and teaches all about quilting. They even answer online questions from beginner and intermediate quilters. They discuss machine quilting, too. Granted it's a break from the tedious and time-consuming hand stitching, but it helps with the piecing together of the blocks. The staff at IQS will help you start off easy with their block of the month project. Quilting is a steady process that requires a careful hand. The shop has quilters who will help you along in the quilting process should you get stuck. And they can help you finish your work should you be in a rush to get the quilt done in time for a special occasion. They are accomplished seamstresses as well as quilters and are involved in bridal and formal sewing commissions, so they know their way around sewing machines—regular and longarm. They can help you with selecting pattern and fabric to make sure your project looks fantastic.

Kennedy Redware, CERAMICS/POTTERY, 10 N. Market St., Muncy 17754; (570) 546-6695; facebook.com/kennedyredware. Studio open by appointment only. Selinda Kennedy opened her Muncy studio in 1986 and developed a signature line of redware pottery employing 17th-, 18th-, and 19th-century motifs. Her designs are inspired by Pennsylvania Dutch folk art found in museums and private collections. These traditional designs are derived primarily from German folk art imagery, song and book plate vignettes, powder horn engravings, *frakturs* (highly artistic and elaborate folk art pieces involving lettering and designs created by the Pennsylvania Dutch), and more.

Using a terra-cotta clay body, Selinda decorates her pieces with colorful food-safe slips, engobes (thinner mixtures than slip), and glazes. Each color is formulated and applied with brushes and sponges, and then detail is applied with a fine brush. She uses slab construction in a variety of sizes and shapes as the canvas. The pieces are fired as soon as they are formed, then are glazed and fired again. Based on research of period designs she combines her own color palette and detail with brushes and glazes. They are signature stamped on the back. Selinda began her career as a redware specialist after taking classes in pottery and then applying for an artist-in-residence program through the Margaret Waldron Foundation. Waldron was a philanthropist whose legacy benefits the community of Muncy.

Penn Woods Pottery, CERAMICS/POTTERY, 102 West Penn St., Muncy 17756; (570) 916-4219. Debbie Leonard works in Pennsylvania German Redware, which is a type of pottery with a burnt-orange/red (think terra-cotta) finish. Inscribed in her clay creations are folk art symbols of birds, animals, flowers, and sometimes people or stylized patterns. This form of pottery dates back to pre-Colonial Pennsylvania, even before William Penn, but the term applies to any common clay pottery that's reddish in color and is fired at lower temps. Debbie inherited her love of pottery from her parents. Upon their retirement, they wanted to have something to share that would create a little joy. After visiting a pottery shop in Virginia and watching patrons personalize their handmade items, her parents opened a similar shop in Muncy. Clients come in, throw pottery, paint their names, and generally have a party. There were a lot of smiles, until, sadly, Debbie's parents passed away. She carried on the tradition and soon began to explore redware. This terra cotta clay captured her heart. And that's all she does. She's willing to depart from the typical Pennsylvania Dutch symbols and designs from time to time. Don't be surprised if you find a charming snowman on some of her work.

McKean

Laughing Owl Press, PAPER/STATIONERY, 27 Fraley St., Kane 16735; (814) 561-1191; laughingowlpress.com. Open Mon through Fri, 10 a.m. to 5 p.m.; Sat by appointment. Laughing Owl is a small letterpress print shop that provides specialty paper items for memorable occasions that need more than just impersonal words and ordinary stock. The term *letterpress* means that the letters and images are pressed or embossed onto the paper stock so that the ink is below the surface. They take a break from the usual business cards and invitations and make coasters, stem tags, and all sorts of customized shapes. Their 3D paper campsite, complete with RV, pine trees, and campfire is worthy of a trip to Kane to see in person. They started letterpress printing about six years ago. Both Joe and Andrea Lanich had great jobs (Andrea was an architect and Joe was a robotics engineer) and were living in New Jersey. Andrea enjoyed designing wedding invitations for friends, and thought it might be nice to get a small printing press. They took a trip to what turned out to be their mentor's print shop in Frenchtown, New Jersey. He had been printing for decades and introduced them to the world of letterpress. They found the first two printing presses on Craigslist and brought them home and set up a shop in their garage. For the next three years, they spent time developing the business and working on their printing skills. By the end of 2011, they knew they could make their hobby a full-time career, but only if they moved back home. So in March 2012 they returned to the wilds of Pennsylvania, where the cost of living was more affordable. Andrea and Joe have established their business, started a family, and simply like the area. Both have both been working full time with the Laughing Owl and have recently hired two more employees. Letterpress printing is totally different from digital printing. Because the printing process leaves an impression in the paper, which you can feel, it adds a very distinctive "touch" to things like wedding invitations. Brides looking for letterpress praise Laughing Owl's customer service, competitive pricing, and quality.

Sign Design of Westline, SIGN DESIGN, 45 Kinzua Pkwy., Mount Jewett 16740; (814) 778-5872. Open Mon through Fri, 9 a.m. to 5 p.m. If you travel along Route 6 in Pennsylvania, it's hard to miss Jerry Clark's work. Since 1980 Jerry has been providing hand-carved and conventionally fabricated signs, storefronts, trade show displays, and vehicle identifications in the area. Sign Design of Westline is located in the middle of the Allegheny National Forest; clients include major hospitals, the medical community, the national and state forestry departments, oil and gas companies, retailers, and companies in the service sector. Jerry is a US Army veteran with an attitude of, "I can't wait to get to the [work] shop." He did the "Welcome to McKean County," "Welcome to Kane," and the "Westline Inn" signs. If he's not in the shop, Jerry is out on the Kinzua Valley Trail, a hike, bike, and ski trail that hooks up in the Kinzua Bridge State Park and the National Recreation Area at Red Bridge. Jerry is the founding president of the Kinzua Bridge Foundation and Kinzua Valley Trail Club.

Zippo, LIGHTERS, 1932 Zippo Dr., Bradford 16701; (814) 368-1932; zippo.com. Open Mon through Sat, 9 a.m. to 5 p.m.; Sun, 11 a.m. to 4 p.m. If you long for the days when people raised lighters instead of cell phones at concerts, come explore the 15,000-square-foot attraction that includes the world-famous Zippo repair clinic and Zippo flagship store. Fourteen custom-made Zippo street lighters line the drive leading up to the building. A 40-foot Zippo lighter with pulsating neon flame towers over the entrance. Enjoy a free self-guided tour where you will learn the rich history of this American icon. Zippo has produced over 400 million windproof lighters since its founding in 1932. Except for improvements in the flint wheel and modifications in case finishes, Blaisdell's original design remains unchanged. The lifetime guarantee that accompanies every Zippo lighter still promises that, "It works or we fix it free."

Mercer

Blommer Chocolate, CANDY/CHOCOLATE, 1101 Blommer Dr., East Greenville 18041; (215) 679-4472 or (800) 825-8181; blommer.com. **Hours vary, call ahead.** Blommer is the largest cocoa processor and ingredient chocolate supplier in North America. This is *the* place to go to buy cocoa powder, cocoa, or milk and dark chocolate chunks for your intricate recipes that absolutely need the best ingredients. And with Blommer's ingredients, it's easy to please fussy eaters. Since 1939 they have been perfecting all things related to the cocoa bean. They are also a leader in sustainable cocoa farming. They are involved in the World Cocoa Foundation, which promotes principles of balanced and sustainable cocoa farming in countries such as the Côte d'Ivoire, Indonesia, and Ecuador. Blommer also sponsors international philanthropic projects, partnering to promote education (they recently opened a primary school in the Côte d'Ivoire). In essence, Blommer Chocolate acts as managers of the product that graces all sorts of confections and desserts for all of North America and elsewhere. As chocolate suppliers they sell to consumers and wholesalers on domestic and international levels. The best part of being your own chocolate supplier is that you can make your own. The Signature Line is an exclusive assortment of milk and dark chocolates that are enveloped with milk, dark, and/or white chocolate coatings.

Daffin Candies and Chocolate Kingdom, CANDY/CHOCOLATE, 496 East State St., Sharon 16146; (724) 342-2892 or (877) 323-3465; daffins.com. **Open Mon through Sat, 9 a.m. to 9 p.m.; Sun, 11 a.m. to 5 p.m.** The world's largest candy store, Daffin Candies has nearly 100 years of experience and three generations in the fine art of candy making. George Daffin started the original family store in 1903 in Ohio. After World War I, George's son Alec took over the business. After Alec's death in 1936, George moved the store to Canton, where his son Paul took over the operations with the help of his mother Georgia. In 1947, armed with merchandising experience and a whole lot of chutzpah, they opened a small downtown store. It served as a factory for creating the delectable candy delights that made the Daffin name famous. Paul's son Pete took over and, with help from wife Jean, the company rose to a whole new level. They also enlisted the help of a friend and created their now famous Peter Rabbit. As demand for Daffin's candy soared, they moved their location to a bigger 20,000-square-foot store in Sharon. At the same time they built a new 30,000-square-foot candy factory in the neighboring town of Farrell. The retail store in Sharon includes large chocolate animals, two large castles, and an entire miniature village with chocolate houses and railroads. The factory in Farrell offers tours of its facilities. Sadly, Pete Daffin passed away in 1998, but the business is now run by Jean. Each piece of Daffin's candy continues to be hand-decorated, a rarity in the candy business.

Emmett's Orchard and Mill House, FARMS 1351 Enterprise Rd., Grove City 16127; (814) 786-7315; emmettsorchard.blogspot.com. Seasonal hours are Tues through Sat, 9 a.m. to 5 p.m. Check website for details. Absolutely, they have apples and cider, but Emmett's hums along to the old bridal verse, "something old, something new, something borrowed, something blue." Their something old is a stone apple butter house; their something new is a wind machine to help fight the frost. The wind machine isn't a fan that cools, but one that pulls the warmer air down, raising the temperature around the branches of the trees a few degrees. This warmer air can save crops from damaging cold. Their something borrowed is the land. Joe and Rachelle Emmett admit the orchard began as a dream in 1997 with a goal of using the old farm in some special way. They wanted to work at something that would keep them together as a family. For them, it was apples. And it's a time-consuming business—apple trees can be temperamental. Although there are many things to be done on the farm, they're happy to know that their children, the next generation, will continue the dream. Their something blue is the Pennsylvania sky in the fall, when the apples are ready to be harvested. Emmett's offers several varieties of apples, cider, and home-baked goodies.

Philadelphia Candies, CANDY/CHOCOLATE, 1546 E State St., Hermitage 16148; (724) 981-6341; philadelphiacandies.com. Open Mon through Sat, 9 a.m. to 9 p.m.; Sun, 11 a.m. to 5 p.m. Full disclosure: Philadelphia Candies is not located in Philadelphia. In 1919, brothers Jim and Steve Macris traveled from Greece to western Pennsylvania's Shenango Valley. They chose to name their business Philadelphia Candies because in their native Greek language the name means *candies made with brotherly love*. In 1939 brothers Louis and John joined Jim and Steve to make and sell chocolates. In 1961, after massive flooding (and before a dam was constructed to control the Shenango River), they moved the business from Sharon to Heritage and built a storefront and factory. In 1965 they introduced a line of chocolate Easter Bunny shapes, dubbed Philly Bunny. This now-essential Easter candy actually made its debut decades before—sometime in the late 1800s and probably in New York City. But bunnies in Pennsylvania didn't catch on until the candy mold technology was firmly in place. (About 76 percent of Americans start nibbling on the poor bunny's ears.) Today, the Macris family still operates Philadelphia Candies' kitchen using fresh ingredients, and they still experiment with molds and candy-making techniques.

Monroe

Barley Creek Brewing Company, BREWERY, 1774 Sullivan Tr., Tannersville 18372; (570) 629-9399; barleycreek.com. Open Mon through Thurs, 11 a.m. to 10:30 p.m.; Fri and Sat, 11 a.m. to 11 p.m.; Sun, 11 a.m. to 10:30 p.m. According to legend, the owners of Barley Creek toiled for a decade on Wall Street, learning all they could about business, finance, and British drinking songs, before the idea came to them in a vision quest: Why make money when you could make beer? That's when they traded briefcases for brewkettles and, in 1995, opened Barley Creek, the first brewpub in northeast Pennsylvania since Prohibition. While owners

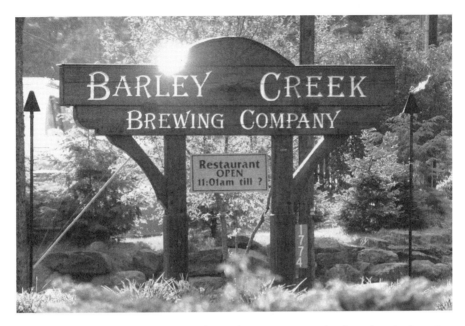

Trip and Eileen Ruvane don't take themselves very seriously, they do take brewing seriously. Over the past 20 years, they've brewed more than 100 different styles of beer, including Brown Antler Ale, Navigator Golden Ale, Iron Arm Wheat, and Rescue IPA. They also produce seasonal ales and single batch brews for special occasions. Barley Creek offers free tours of their working brewhouse every day, with free tastings for guests over 21. To celebrate its first 20 years in business, Barley Creek is now tapping into a new type of brewing. Plans are underway to add a craft distillery onsite, where they will brew small batches of vodka, moonshine, gin, rum, whiskey, and other spirits. Guests are always in for a unique experience, whether they come to Barley Creek for the craft beer and spirits, the great food, or the outdoor Pint Size Park complex, where they can play wiffleball, cornhole, and something called Firkin Curling, another Pennsylvania invention (think curling, only with mini beer kegs).

Meatloaf's Kitchen, PETS, Canadensis 18325; (570) 676-3627; meatloafsdog treats.com. A small business inspired by a big love of dogs, one in particular called Meatloaf, who had a pretty tough start in life. He was a stray puppy, rescued in the middle of a four-lane highway, shivering and lost. His forever-home parents found out he had food allergies and could only eat certain kinds of dog food and treats. So his owner, Melanie Stracko (who's a trained pastry chef), decided his treats had to be homemade. After Meatloaf started sharing, Meatloaf's Kitchen became a small business. They make fresh homemade dog treats, specializing in vegan and vegetarian. All their dog treats are made fresh when you place your order. They are never frozen and contain no preservatives or unhealthy chemicals. Their amazing treats are shaped into cinnamon buns, cupcakes, lobsters, pretzels, and more—all the things you know your best friend loves but really should not be eating. MK's treats are available online and at Monroe Farmer's Market (Sat 8:00 a.m. to noon) and Milford Farmer's Market (Sun 10:00 a.m. to 2:00 p.m.).

Mountain Knits & Pearls, KNITTING/BEADING, 114 East Washington St., East Stroudsburg 18301; (570) 424-7770; mtnknitspearls.com. Open Tues, 10 a.m. to 8:30 p.m.; Wed through Fri, 10 a.m. to 5 p.m.; and Sat, 9 a.m. to 9 p.m. This little shop of delights combines fiber arts with beadwork. This mixed media starts with yarn and knitting. It blends beads within the strands of the knit.

It sounds very new, but is an art form that comes from the Native Americans, who embellished their clothes and nearly every type of functional piece they used to all manner of everyday and ceremonial artwork. Joanne Deardoff owns Mountain Knits & Pearls and appreciates the Native American love of found object arts—from pebble to wooden beads to feathers, and all sorts of fibers and fur. Joanne also teaches knitting, and in one class she was able to show her class, men included, how to make small doll sweaters. These are a great starter project that can be adjusted to dog sweaters, toddler sweaters, and, eventually with a bit more yarn, a sweater for yourself or a loved one. Joanne also supplies the beginner to advanced crocheter with all their crocheting accessories.

Summer Kitchen Soaps, SOAP, 3139 Turkey Hill Rd., Stroudsburg 18360; (570) 992-5534; summerkitchensoaps.com. Michelle Harps lives on a small farm in a rural part of the Pocono Mountains with her husband Paul and the youngest of their five children. While discussing ways to earn extra income from the farm, they kicked around the idea of raising goats. Anticipating an abundance of goat's milk, Michelle tried to think of ways to utilize the surplus. She began her list: goat cheese, yogurt, fudge, and soap. First things first, she had to experiment and see if she could actually create any of these products successfully. She tried soap first and was hooked after the first batch. Then she started experimenting with different scents and ingredients. She unapologetically used her family and enthusiastic co-workers (at her other job) as guinea pigs. Everyone loved them so much that she started making them for Christmas gifts. People purchased them because *they* wanted to give them as gifts, too. Many of her soaps are natural, and many are vegan, except those made with goat's milk, honey, or beeswax. She uses only high-quality, vegetable-based oils with the exception of the "Old Fashioned Grandma's Lard Soap," and what self-respecting mistress of soaps (aka "soapstress") would leave that one out? A list of retailers is available online.

Montgomery

Castle Studio, Inc., GLASS, 1333 East Prospect Ave., North Wales 19454; (215) 699-0400; castlestudioinc.com. Call ahead for hours. Located outside of Philadelphia, Castle Studio Stained Glass is a full-service studio accomplished at performing any requirements in the field of stained glass. They are proficient in the creation of new designs, both modern and traditional, as well as the restoration of older stained glass windows and their frames. In addition their unique designs in protective glazing systems generate a significantly greater venting area than other systems offered in the market today. With over 20 years of experience, they offer expert advice throughout the stained glass process so customers can feel at ease and make informed decisions throughout their projects. Castle Studio recently completed an art glass restoration project at the historic Elstowe Manor in Elkins Park, outside of Philadelphia. This project entailed the complete restoration of one stained glass ceiling in the mansion, as well as the cleaning of a second ceiling. Details of this extensive project have been documented in a booklet that explains the steps taken to restore these beautiful windows to their original grandeur.

Lehigh Valley Dairy Farms, DAIRY, 880 Allentown Rd., Lansdale 19446; (215) 855-8205; lehighvalleydairyfarms.com. For more than 70 years, Lehigh Valley Dairy Farms has brought residents milks, creams, and juices. From humble beginnings on a small family farm in Lansdale, Pennsylvania, Lehigh Valley has grown over the years, but they remain true to their small farm roots. And they look forward to many more years of growing within the dairy business. The Lansdale facility is home to more than 360 dedicated dairy operations workers, sales and merchandising personnel, and delivery drivers. Not just for the Lehigh Valley region, they provide dairy products to communities in Delaware, Maryland, New Jersey, New York, Virginia, and West Virginia. Their corporate headquarters are located in Lansdale, but they have facilities and distribution centers in Schuylkill, Haven, and Allentown, as well as in Delaware and New Jersey. They are a subsidiary of Dean Foods, one of the largest processors and direct-to-store distributors of fluid milk, and their products are found in the dairy refrigerators at Acme, Giant, Walmart, Target, Super Fresh, and Walgreens. Their website also has recipes that use—you guessed it— milk as a chief ingredient. Hint: Their sweet potato biscuits recipe is a winner.

Nutmeg Designs, MOSAICS, P.O. Box 675, Lansdale 19446; (215) 353-6970; nutmegdesignsart.com. When Margaret Almon lost her job, it was a very good thing. A door opened and she followed her artistic passion. After viewing a mosaic by Hildreth Meière at the Jesuit Center in Wernersville, she immediately fell in love with the technique—the intricate patterns, light-catching sparkle, and breathtaking composition. Husband Wayne Stratz, a stained-glass artisan (his works appear on the website, too), already had many spare pieces of glass for Margaret to utilize. The more she experimented, the more certain she became that creating with mosaic would truly make her happy. Mosaics are typically created by taking small, colored pieces of hard material, such as glass, and arranging them together to form a picture or pattern. Mortar is used to hold the pieces in place—like tiles on

a bathroom floor. Margaret uses Pennsylvania-made materials, slate from the Slate Belt of eastern Pennsylvania for her base, and glass from a manufacturer in the western part of the state. Her favorite (and most popular) pieces are mosaics that are inspirational words and house numbers.

Pierson Plugs, SPORTING EQUIPMENT, 2121 Rahn Ave., Perkiomenville 18074; (215) 234-4404; piersonplugs.com. Open 6 a.m. to 8 p.m. daily. Prop baits are one of the highest rated topwater lures ever made or fished. They're good for large- and small-mouth bass, striped bass, muskie, pike—in fact, they're almost foolproof. These lures are considered by many to be some of the finest handcrafted cedar top water lures in the world today. Bill Pierson, owner of Pierson Plugs, learned from his neighbor and masters alike for over 45 years. At first he hand carved his plugs, but then his wife bought him a lathe to turn plugs instead of hand carving them. He had no one to show him how and what to do, but after some trial and error, he got the knack. He started fishing with them and was quite successful. Friends of his were impressed by his work and started putting orders in. They, too, started doing well with his plugs, and what was a hobby for many years turned into a business in 2005. Throughout the years, Bill has perfected his technique for turning, painting, and assembling the plugs to make them what you see today. He is always coming up with new ideas to keep his creations fresh and interesting by listening to his customers and the ideas of the people who work with him. Bill hopes you'll enjoy his lures, even if you don't decide to fish with them. Because for some, lures are more than something you tie on a fishing line, they're actually collectible items. Bill says there are many years of the love of the sport of fishing and the outdoors put into all the plugs he makes.

Stacie Dale Designs, WOODWORKING, 33 Buckwalter Rd., Audubon 19403; (610) 666-6484. staciedaledesigns.com. Open Mon through Fri, 9 a.m. to 4 p.m. Stacie started her career after receiving a degree in fashion design from Drexel University in 1992. She worked in the apparel industry for nine years and then took some time off when she had her children. She's always loved painting and even painted on clothing for her senior collection in college. She should have known then that painting was her first love. When her friends started having children, she painted toy chests and keepsake chests for them as gifts. It slowly blossomed into a full-time keepsake chest business in 1997. Now she spends her days painting custom keepsake chests, memory boxes, and wall art for babies, weddings, family trees, bereavement, and other special occasions. She has a small studio in the back of her home where she creates pieces to be cherished for generations. Her cabinetmaker Craig Jarvis has a workshop in his basement where he makes all the chests and then delivers them to her storage space a few miles down the road.

Woodstrip Watercraft Co., SPORTING EQUIPMENT, 1818 Swamp Pike, Gilbertsville 19525; (610) 326-9282; woodstrip.whca.org. Open Mon through Fri, 10 a.m. to 6 p.m.; Sat, 10 a.m. to 3 p.m. Alwin Bratton opened Woodstrip Watercraft Co. for business in 1987, building cedarstrip canoes. Kayaks and the restoration of classic wood/canvas canoes and paddlemaking quickly followed. Over the years they've developed new designs and offer custom design services as well as patterns for several of their canoes. And if you are the quintessential DIYer, they sell all the supplies for the canoe-crafter (except wood). Their standard canoes are made of edge-glued strips of cedar, bead and coved, covered with fiberglass cloth and epoxy. The trim (seats, thwarts, gunnels, and decks) is a mix of ash and mahogany. They build each custom boat to order; special requirements can also be built in, as long as they are safe. Their strip kayaks are built in the same manner as their canoes, including fiberglass on the hull and decks, and the bulkheads and trim are made of marine plywood. This construction is light, stiff, and very strong, besides being beautiful. In addition to their canoes and kayaks, in 2002 they started building Adirondack guideboats. These were popular in that region for nearly a century as the main method of travel prior to the road system of today. New from Woodstrip Watercraft is their series of small-decked canoes. Designed to bring the usefulness of the solo canoe in a decked version, these one-man or one-woman canoes are smaller and lighter than most. These boats are ideal for both lake and river paddling, fishing, photography, or just knocking about (in style and class, of course).

Northampton

Barry Gebhart Jewelry, JEWELRY, 2189 Rovaldi Ave., Bethlehem 18015; (610) 691-0687; bgjewelry.com. Hand-hammered, forged Argentium (the good stuff) sterling silver jewelry, plus 35 years of jewelry-making experience equals the creation of must-haves for your jewelry box. You will want to wear this man's art. Barry has created necklaces, pendants, earrings, bracelets, rings, anklets, toe rings, barrettes, and stickpins. He also adorns some of his silver with semiprecious and precious stones. His earrings, pendants, bracelets, and necklaces have appeared in fine retailers in Pennsylvania and Maryland. His American, handmade, tarnish-resistant sterling silver jewelry is even sold at fine retailers as far away as the US Virgin Islands. A native of Bethlehem, he is especially proud of his Moravian Star pendants. The Moravian Star is otherwise known as the *Herrnhut* star. It is most often white and has a multitude of spikes when in its 3D form. It's displayed in homes hanging as a separate decoration or as a tree ornament around Advent or Christmas. Bethlehem, the Christmas City, uses the *Herrnhut* star in the city's logo. And it's no surprise that Barry's Moravian stars are featured at the city's Moravian Book Store.

Capozzolo Brothers Slate Co., SLATE, 1342 Ridge Rd., Bangor 18013; (800) 282-6582; capozzoloslate.com. **Open daily 10 a.m. to 5 p.m.** Slate is as much a part of Pennsylvania history as coal. So rich in the mineral is the northeastern area that it was dubbed the Slate Belt. Quarries opened to harvest slate for chalkboards, roofing shingles, and tiles. Today the versatile and waterproof rock is also used for interior and industrial design as well as crafts and novelty items. But slate was also used in the making of toys, such as pool tables and *quoits*. That's right, *quoits*. Pronounced *kah-wayts*, the game is played by pitching hard rubber rings onto or near aluminum hubs (spikes). It is much like the game of horseshoes in method (two players per side) and scoring (the first team to reach 21 wins). However, the game is more formalized with each ring or quoit weighing 4 pounds. Hubs are mounted on slate boards and the distance between the hubs is 18 feet. Unlike horseshoes, quoits can be played indoors. It's been suggested that the game may have originated among the slate quarry men who grew tired of cracking rocks all day and needed a post-work pastime for amusement. Capozzolo Brothers make and sell rubber quoits, hubs, and slate quoit boards.

C.F. Martin & Co Guitars, MUSICAL INSTRUMENTS, 510 Sycamore St., Nazareth 18064; (610) 759-2837; martinguitar.com. Martin Museum & Visitor Center is open Mon through Fri, 8 a.m. to 5 p.m. Factory tours are offered between 11 a.m. and 2:30 p.m. Ever since the guitar began to take hold in the early 1800s, C.F. Martin has been inextricably intertwined in the guitar's evolution and innovation. Although economic conditions went through periods of instability,

Martin was able to survive the Civil War, World War I, the Great Depression, World War II, and even the disco decade. The formula for Martin's success is and always has been an unparalleled commitment to precise hand-craftsmanship blended with optimum tonewoods and singular design. Today Martin remains the oldest surviving maker of stringed instruments in the world, and the most respected maker of acoustic guitars in America. Martin's most significant innovations include the invention of the X-bracing pattern in 1843, the invention of the Dreadnought guitar design in 1916, the development of the 14-fret neck for acoustic guitars in 1929, plus many dozens of guitar, ukulele, and mandolin shapes and sizes that he originated. In the preface to the 1904 catalog, Frank Henry Martin stated, "A good guitar cannot be built for the price of a poor one, but who regrets the extra cost for a good guitar?" Now, more than a century later, these words still accurately express Martin's ongoing commitment to quality. What was once a one-man shop is now an energy-filled facility with more than 600 skilled employees. The extended Martin family, now and in the future, is fully committed to preserving and extending the vision of C.F. Martin, Sr. by continuing to make the finest acoustic guitars in the world.

Crayola Crayon Factory (Binney & Smith), TOYS AND GAMES. 30 Centre Sq., Easton 18042; (610) 515-8000; binney-smith.com. Open Mon through Fri, 9:30 a.m. to 4 p.m.; Sat and Sun, 10 a.m. to 6 p.m. Founded in 1885, Crayons moved to Pennsylvania because owner Edwin Binney was attracted to the state's slate reserves. Originally started as a chemical company in New York (Peekskill Chemical Works), the company moved across the Delaware River to a new factory in Easton in 1902. Edwin Binney and C. Harold Smith formed a partnership to start making black colorants and introduced the Staonal Marking Crayon. They also introduced the first dustless school chalk. In 1903 the company went to wax and began producing crayons in eight different colors. In 1949, they expanded to 48 colors and then to 64 in 1958. The company was forward thinking as early as 1936, promoting safety in art supplies by becoming a founding member of the Crayon, Watercolor and Craft Institute. This entity certifies and labels craft products as nontoxic. Today the name

Crayola is synonymous with the word *crayons*. They make water-based markers, nontoxic water color paints, and, of course, crayons. And their crayon box has expanded to a 120-color "wheel." Crayola holds an annual "name the new color crayon" contest for kids to be creative, while retiring some not-so-popular shades.

Just Born Candy, CANDY/CHOCOLATE, Bethlehem 18015; (610) 652-5353; peepsandcompany.com. The Just Born candy tradition actually began in 1910 when Sam Born emigrated to the US from Russia. A candymaker by trade, Born used innovative technology to produce chocolate sprinkles, known as Jimmies, and the hard chocolate coating for ice cream bars. In 1916 Born invented a machine that mechanically inserted sticks into lollipops. In 1923 Born opened a small candymaking and retail store in Brooklyn, New York. He marketed the freshness of his line of daily-made candy with a sign that declared, "Just Born." Not long after opening the Brooklyn store, Born invited his brothers-in-law, Irv and Jack Shaffer, to join him in the business. The company thrived in spite of the economic depression of the 1930s and, in 1932, moved its operations to an empty printing factory in Bethlehem, Pennsylvania. The company continued to grow, aided by several key acquisitions. In 1935 Just Born acquired the prestigious Maillard Corporation, well known for elegant hand-decorated chocolates, crystallized fruits, Venetian mints, and jellies. In 1953 Just Born acquired the Rodda Candy Company of Lancaster. Although best known for its jelly beans, Rodda also made marshmallow products that were made by laboriously hand-squeezing marshmallow through pastry tubes. Sam Born's son Bob, who had joined the company in 1946, helped mechanize the marshmallow forming process, and Just Born has become the world's largest manufacturer of novelty marshmallow treats. Other popular products have been introduced over the years including Mike and Ike chewy fruit-flavored candies in 1940, spicy, cinnamon-flavored Hot Tamales in 1950, Teenee Beanee gourmet jelly beans in 1977, and sour Zours in 1999. Just Born Candy can be found at the candy store located at 77 Sands Blvd. in Bethlehem, which is open Sun through Thurs, 10 a.m. to 9 p.m.; Fri and Sat, 10 a.m. to 11 p.m.

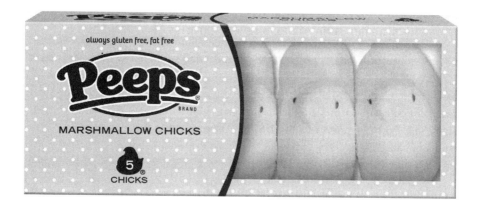

Kraemer Textiles, Inc., TEXTILES, 240 Main St., Nazareth 18064; (610) 759-4030; kraemeryarns.com. **Open Mon through Fri, 9 a.m. to 5 p.m.; Sat 9 a.m. to 4 p.m.** This textile company almost went down for the count as one of the last yarn makers in Pennsylvania, but along came the Olympics. Kramer's was contracted to make the thread for the US Olympic team's uniforms. It wasn't the biggest order of the company's 125-year history, but it was probably one of the most significant. Something warm from Pennsylvania went to one of the coldest places on Earth. Kraemer Yarns of Nazareth spun the wool for Team USA's opening ceremony sweaters at the 2014 Olympic Winter Games in Sochi, Russia. The cardigan sweaters were a deep navy blue with stars sprinkled on the back and sleeves. The front of the sweaters sported a few red and white strips, with a single American flag on the shoulder and bright red "USA" letters on the upper back. The USA Team went on to win 9 gold medals, 7 silver medals, and 12 bronze medals, for a total of 28, second to Russia who won a total of 33 medals. Sometimes it does matter what you're wearing.

Majestic Athletics, APPAREL, 2320 Newlins Mill Rd., Easton 18100; (610) 599-4901; majesticathletic.com. In 1976 Faust Capobianco started a sports apparel manufacturing business. It was his mom's fault. He inherited his passion for the fabric first-hand from his mother Mary who owned a garment company called Maria Rose Fashions, which primarily made women's shirts. Faust moved his company toward men's clothes and sports apparel. His company, Majestic, was always in the "minors" when it came to the production of sports clothing. But he entered the "big leagues" when they began making major league baseball batting jerseys. And then they signed a licensing agreement that meant only Majestic was permitted to make MLB-approved jerseys for the MLB players during batting practice. In 2005 Majestic became the sole provider of authentic jerseys for all 30 MLB teams. They are also licensed to commercialize uniforms and clothing of most of the main sports teams in the US and Canada. That ensures Majestic can produce and sell professional baseball, basketball, football, and hockey clothes to you. The players' true uniforms that they wear for games are licensed to other companies such as Nike, Reebok, and Adidas. The great thing is that you can custom order from the same company who outfits your sports' heroes. Majestic makes more than 1 million jerseys per year, many of which can be found at their retail shop at 2198 Industrial Dr. in Bethlehem (610-814-2650), which is open Saturday from noon until 6 p.m.

Red-Tail Designs, JEWELRY, Easton 18042; (610) 905-8399; redtaildesigns .com. Susan Newquist can get a bit prickly—she works with porcupine quills, so that's to be expected. Truth be told, Susan is a gentle person whose heart is intertwined with her love of the ancient arts. She also works with horse hair and utilizes both quill and hair as a nod to the artistry of the original Pennsylvanians, the Lenni Lenape Native Americans. This tribe spanned across three states—Pennsylvania, New Jersey, and Delaware—and are still represented by a council in Pennsylvania. The quill of a porcupine and the tail hair of a horse are actually similar in make-up— both contain keratin—although vastly different in thickness and sharpness. Native American women would pull quills from a pelt after a hunt or toss a blanket over the porcupine and harvest the quills that stuck in the blanket. The quills were cleaned, flattened, sometimes dyed, and embroidered onto leather or other media. Susan gathers her own horsehair or accepts hair from a client's horse to weave it into bracelets, cuffs, necklaces, or earrings. She offers monogramming on requested metal plates with the name of the horse, if desired. She embellishes the jewelry with clasps, beads, and gemstones. Susan's creations can be found at The Arts Barn at 3 Berry Rd. in Schuylkill Haven.

Weyerbacher Brewing Company, BREWERY, 905 Line St., Easton 18042; (610) 559-5561; weyerbacher.com. Open Mon through Fri, 10 a.m. to 7 p.m. Dan Weirbach should be a happy man—his brewery distributes to practically the entire eastern seaboard and beyond. His wife Sue has been by his side every step of the way. He has received accolades on his brews, but that wasn't good enough, he wants more. In fact he dreams of a day when every beer distributor has his beer displayed. Dan and Sue opened Weyerbacher in a livery stable in downtown Easton in August 1995. It wasn't until 1997, with the release of their first big beer, Raspberry Imperial Stout (one of Dan's favorite homebrew recipes), that people began to take notice. The following year, Blithering Idiot Barley wine was introduced. Then they began brewing Belgian beers, one called Merry Monks Ale. They took the road not traveled and made full-flavored, high-quality brews for the discerning customer. With clever names like Tart Noveau, Wit, and Last Chance IPA, you know their beers aren't your run-of-the-mill craft brews. And just in case you were curious, *Weyerbacher* (*wire-bach-ker*) was the original spelling of the Weirbach family name, used by the first immigrants from Germany about 200 years ago. The spelling has morphed slightly over time.

Northumberland

Sunbury Textile Mills, TEXTILES, 1200 Miller St., Sunbury 17801; (570) 286-3800; sunburytextiles.com. Open Mon through Fri, 9 a.m. to 5 p.m. For many years this mill has been operating underneath its signature sawtooth roof. It is now one of the last mills in the country. Sunbury is known for its decorative jacquards used in the hospitality industries, and for the Sunbrella brand of sturdy outdoor fabrics. The sawtooth design was to shield the factory workers from direct sunlight but still allow natural light to illuminate as much of the factory as possible. Modern electric-powered looms moved into the building around the 1970s, but the roof remained. It's now lauded for its energy-efficient design. Sunbury also recycles over 250 tons of yarn waste and cardboard annually. They use no water in the making of their fabrics. And they even recycle customers' used computers and monitors. The company also has a showroom in New York City that features their latest fabrics and designs.

Perry

Blue Mountain Outfitters, SPORTING EQUIPMENT, 103 South State Rd., Marysville 17053; (717) 957-2143; bluemountainoutfitters.net. Open Mon through Sat, 10 a.m. to 8 p.m. In the early 1980s, Blue Mountain Outfitters operated out of a much smaller shop, next to a chiropractor's office. The doctor's clients commented about the strange smells wafting out of the fiberglass repair shop, which was also the showroom, store, and office. Doug Gibson, owner and president, has helped the company grow from a small canoe rental business to a full-service, year-round paddlesports shop. Still, they're always on the lookout for anything new, exciting, unique, and sometimes odd in the paddlesports world. They admit they still produce strange smells from their ever-improving repair and outfitting shop, usually experimenting with some new repair materials or techniques, but now Blue Mountain Outfitters is in a landmark—the historic Marysville Train Station, built at the turn of last century. At about the same time, another area landmark was being constructed downstream on the Susquehanna—the Rockville Bridge, the longest stone arch bridge in the world. The Marysville Station served as a hub of the Pennsylvania Railroad in the capitol region until passenger service was discontinued in the mid-1950s. Needing to sell off the declining station, it was first offered to the Borough of Marysville for a sum of $1, but the offer was turned down. A lengthy period of revolving ownership and uses followed, including a lumberyard, an antiques shop, an optician's shop, a small-engine repair shop, and the one most remembered, a drive-through beer distributor. Blue Mountain Outfitters purchased the building in 1992. You'll still find evidence of the old Pennsylvania Railroad Days, and maybe a beer bottle or two (from the distributor days, of course), but today it is a true paddler's shop.

Hall's Ice Cream, DAIRY, 861 Raccoon Valley Rd., Millerstown 17062, (717) 589-3290; hallsicecream.com Open daily from June to August typically 3 to 9 p.m. Only opened on weekends rest of the year. Around 1905, while still living within the limits of Millerstown, William J. Hall began selling milk from a metal can and ladle hauled to town by a horse-drawn buggy. Shortly after moving a few miles outside of town to "Pleasant Home Farm," rumor has it that he bought the last remaining cow in town. Not long after, he purchased a specially constructed delivery

wagon from Swab Wagon Co. in Elizabethville for the purpose of delivering milk. There was a spigot for dispensing the milk, and a stirring rod to keep the milk from separating. William Hall continued selling milk from his wagon until 1916, when his health failed and he had to quit. Several of Mr. Hall's neighbors began delivering milk to replace his business in Raccoon Valley. In 1926, James Beaver of Little Pfoutz Valley began the first delivery of milk in glass bottles under the name Echo Glen Dairy. In 1939, William's son John K. Hall along with his sons, John Allen, William (Bill), and James (Jim), built a plant at the Pleasant Home Farm site and were the first to introduce pasteurized milk to the area. Eight years later in 1947, they were the first in the area to begin homogenizing milk. Also in 1947, John Allen began manufacturing ice cream, having taken a short course at Penn State University. The milk and ice cream business continued at this location until John's death in 1964. The business then merged with Miller Brothers' Dairy in Millersburg and John Allen remained as manager and ice cream maker at the Millerstown location. In 1982, Miller Brothers' sold the milk business to Harrisburg Dairies and the ice cream remained with John Allen. He continued to make his trademark ice cream until his health began to fail in 1994, at which time his son and daughter, Allen and Margaret (Peggy Hall) Raub, took over the operation. These days Hall's Ice Cream can be found in Perry, Juniata, Mifflin, Snyder, Dauphin, Cumberland, and Adams counties. Hall's makes over 40 flavors of premium (14 percent butterfat), Premium Honey (14 percent butterfat and 8 percent PA Preferred Honey), lite, and no-sugar added ice creams, and several flavors of sherbet. They can customize flavors or put ice cream in molds for special events such as weddings, anniversaries, or birthdays.

Philadelphia

Amoroso's, FOOD/BAKERY, 845 South 55th St., Philadelphia 19143; (215) 471-4740; amorosobaking.com. Open Mon through Fri, 9 a.m. to 5 p.m. Vincenzo

Amoroso arrived in New Jersey in 1904 and almost immediately started a bakery—doing what he loved to do with his sons Salvatore and Joseph. His family outgrew their small bakery in Camden, New Jersey, and moved across the river to Philly in 1914. In 1929, despite the Great Depression, the bakery survived by making deliveries, often twice a day. Sons Daniel, Vincent, Leonard, and Sal joined the bakery, helping out before and after school. They increased the area they serviced and by the 1950s were delivering to restaurants, grocery stores, and supermarkets. The bakery then expanded to its present location on South 55th Street. Undergoing five major expansions, Amoroso Baking goes coast to coast with their products. With the technology of freezing "par baked" rolls, Amoroso's can now fly to other countries and be enjoyed after full baking. After having celebrated its 100th anniversary, they're happy to stay family-owned and -operated. Hint: These are the best rolls for cheesesteaks—just sayin'.

Anvil Iron Works, IRONWORKS, 1022-26 Washington Ave., Philadelphia 19147; (215) 468-8300; anviliron.net. Open Mon through Fri, 7:30 a.m. to 4 p.m.; Sat, 8 a.m to noon. The City of Brotherly Love is alive with an art form as solid as its history. Anvil Iron designs, manufactures, and installs interior and exterior ornamental wrought iron. It's believed that the first iron forge in the colony of Pennsylvania was established by blacksmith Thomas Rutter in the late 1600s. Anvil Iron works is a third-generation, family-owned and -operated business that has served residential and business clients in the Philadelphia area since 1940. The work they've done ranges from services for the smallest row home in South Philly to ornamental ironwork for Lincoln Financial Field. The "Linc" is the sports stadium that replaced the Veterans Stadium, an icon of sports arenas, after the Vet was demolished in 2004. Lincoln Field is home to the football teams of the Temple University Owls, the Philadelphia Eagles, and temporary home to the Philadelphia Union (soccer). It has also hosted three Bruce Springsteen concerts.

Bassetts Ice Cream, DAIRY, 1211 Chestnut St., Philadelphia 19107; (215) 864-2771; bassettsicecream.com. Open Mon through Fri, 9 a.m. to 6 p.m.; Sat, 8

a.m. to 6 p.m.; Sun, 9 a.m. to 5 p.m. One of America's oldest ice cream shops thrives downtown. In 1861 Quaker school teacher and farmer L. D. Bassett opened an ice cream shop across the river, but then moved his business to Market Street in 1885. Even before the age of refrigeration, Bassett was able to churn ice cream and keep it cool in icehouses. Needless to say, the wonderfully creamy taste has garnered rave reviews from the local foodie folks who are pretty particular when it comes to desserts. There are over 30 flavors from which to choose, including seasonal favorites. For the hungry traveler there's a Bassetts store in the Reading Terminal Market (where production was moved in 1892), selling ice cream in a cone, dish, or to go container. But you don't have to travel to Philly to enjoy a spoonful of Pomegranate Blueberry Chunk; you can go online and order your favorite flavor. Bassetts Ice Cream will celebrate 155 years of sweet coolness in 2016. The Bassett family members—fifth generation (we're talking: great, great grand) are still involved in the day-to-day functioning of the company's brand and flavor development.

Beekman's C.O.P.A. Soaps, SOAPS, 438 East Girard Ave., Philadelphia, 19125; (215) 426-5594 or (800) 315-5690; copasoaps.com. Open by appointment only. These soaps are cold processed in the Philadelphia shop. While their shop is small, their appeal is grand. Fans from all over ask for their scented suds. These soap makers use the oils that the name stands for, C is for coconut, O is for olive, P is for palm, and A is for almond. Owners Toni and Dave have over a dozen different types of soaps and skin products that feel and smell luxurious. Their most popular scent is lavender, including their Lavender Shea with Honey soap. And it's tough to leave their shop with just one bar, so it makes sense to stock up while you're in Philly. But if you can't, their online presence with an ordering option is a lifesaver. Plus, shipping is free!

Bluecoat American Dry Gin, DISTILLERY, Philadelphia Distilling Company, 12285 McNulty Rd., Philadelphia 19154; (215) 671-0346; bluecoatgin.com. Tours offered on Sat, 2 and 4 p.m. During the American Revolution, the British soldiers were given the nickname "redcoats" referring to the bright red uniforms they wore. The Colonists went contrary and dubbed their Continental Army "bluecoats." This gin's name is a nod to the history of Pennsylvania and the city where the distillery is located. The bottle's bright blue color stands out as much as the contents. Admittedly the colonies aren't necessarily known for their dry gin— beer yes, but the fermented product of juniper berries, not so much. This distillery creates small batches of distilled gin in copper pots and finished in oak barrels for at least three months—a labor-intensive process. It produces a unique gin that's just as good in martinis as it is in gin and tonics. Typically gins are best for one and not the other. You can taste the gin's spices of cardamom and citrus, which is a nice departure from gins that are so dry they evaporate before the olive is added to the martini glass. This gin can be found all over the city and is available in a dozen states.

Cicada Leather Company, LEATHER, 4919 Pentridge St., Philadelphia 19113; Cicada leathercompany@gmail.com; cicadaleathercompany.com. Mia Barrett is a Martha Stewart atelier finalist. That means her studio's floor is covered with leather scraps and that her work is exceptional. She learned the basics of leathercraft in a high school art class and fell in love. She loves that leather is a unique medium. It's durable and able to withstand harsh weather and rough handling. And rather than fall apart with continued use, leather only gains personality. She says that leather ages and evolves with the owner. A treasured leather item tells a story of your life. She should know. She designs and creates leather goods—wallets, camera straps, leather bags, belts, jewelry, and more. Because leather is porous, it absorbs oils, so when you hold a leather wallet that she's created, it takes in the oils of the handler (you) and in a sense, becomes more like you. The more you use your leather item, the more uniquely like you it becomes. Mia uses traditional tools and methods to create products that last for years. Her items are hand-stitched using a stitching method that is stronger than those from sewing machines. Don't be puzzled by the "bug" on her logo. Cicadas are the symbol of hope and wisdom. She shares her passion for leather by holding workshops in her studio. And you can keep whatever you create.

East Falls Glassworks, GLASS, 3510 Scotts Ln., Philadelphia 19129; (215) 908-7924; eastfallsglass.com. Open Mon through Fri, 10 a.m. to 6 p.m. Call ahead for Sat and Sun hours. This is the city's largest studio and gallery dedicated to hot glass. The glassblowing studio is located minutes from the Philadelphia Art Museum, which is a one-of-a-kind museum that houses pieces of large glass work, a testament to the city's love of all artistic media. Glassblowing requires silica (sand) to be superheated and gathered at the end of a blowpipe (long hollow pole). The glass at this stage is similar to the consistency of caramel. The glassblower pushes air down through the tube and "inflates" the glass at the end as if blowing up a balloon. He or she then takes the piece to a work bench and shapes it or goes back to gather more glass, which can add color and texture to the original piece. Once the piece is cut from the blowpipe it's cooled.

Geno's Steaks, MEAT, 1219 South 9th St., Philadelphia 19147; (215) 389-0659; genosteaks.com. Open 24 hours. This cheesesteak shop is directly across the street form Pat's. Geno's Steaks was started by Joey Vento in 1966. He figured if he was going to sell cheesesteaks, it needed to be where they were already eating them—at the X-shaped intersection of 9th & Passyunk in South Philly. Joey learned the ropes of the cheesesteak business from his father who, in the early 1940s, opened a steak shop named "Jim's Steaks" across the street from where Geno's now stands. In 1966 Joey started Geno's with two boxes of steaks, some hot dogs, and $6 in his pocket. Since there was already a "Joe's Steaks," he had to come up with a new name. He noticed a broken door in the back of his store on which the name "Gino" had been painted. Joey liked the name but back then there was already a food chain by that name. He changed the "i" to an "e" and proceeded to name his steak shop Geno's Steaks. In 1971, when his son was born, Joey and his wife Eileen decided to name him after their business. Geno Vento worked alongside his father from the age of 17 until Joey's passing in 2011. Geno continues to work hard every day to make his father proud and continue the cheesesteak legacy. The ingredients are simple and never greasy: thinly sliced rib-eye steak, melted cheese, oven-baked bread, and grilled onions. Awaiting your piping-hot sandwich on the counter outside are ketchup, mustard, and relish.

Greg Stefan Studios—Stained Glass, GLASS, 2193 Pratt St., Philadelphia 19124; (215) 929-1309; gregstefan.com. Call ahead for studio hours. Greg Stefan has been creating in stained glass from the age of 10, when he first learned how to cut stained glass. In the beginning, it was just a hobby, but then it turned into a seven-plus-year apprenticeship where he mastered the craft of restoring, repairing, designing, and fabricating beautiful stained glass windows. Greg attended Bucks County Community College for business administration and opened his first studio and design center and showroom in Bensalem-Andalusia in 2005. He's also served as a journeyman and job foreman for stained glass companies such as Willet Hauser Architectural and Femenella & Associates. In 2013 Greg Stefan Studios relocated to the East Frankford section of Philadelphia. The new facility includes a machine shop, supply floor, classroom, and shop. Greg currently resides in Bucks County. His works have been displayed and sold across the US, England, Australia, France, and Poland. Greg has taught and shared his passion with hundreds of students for over 10 years. He offers in-house workshops, clinics, and stained glass classes ranging from novice to the advanced historical restoration level.

The Hex Factory, HEX SIGNS, 2080 E. Cumberland St., Philadelphia, 19125; (917) 375-4982 or (215) 688-6285; thehexfactory.com. Studio visits by appointment. Hunter Yoder paints round signs. You may think that a single shape limits his creativity. On the contrary, for him, the possibilities are endless. Yoder paints hex signs, and he specializes in pre-Christian signs. The type of imagery and symbolism that pre-dates William Penn's settlement. Yoder's theory is that the German immigrants brought with them symbols of pre-Germanic

pagan art that, once on this side of the Atlantic, evolved into hex signs. It's ironic that a very rigid Christian sect used non-Christian art to develop its own symbols of luck and fertility. Yoder is also a hexologist, which means he's like the "CSI" of hex signs and barnstars. Hexsigns are more than decorations to him. Yoder can tell the history of a barn's owner and the surrounding area just by looking at the pattern and the colors on a sign. True, there aren't many barns in Philly, but less than a half hour away he can show you authentic examples of this very-Pennsylvanian folk art. He knows the area well and can trace 10 generations of his own family line that live and died in Pennsylvania Dutch Country.

Humphrys Flag Company, Inc., FLAGS, 238 Arch St., Philadelphia 19106; (800) 227-3524; humphrysflag.com. Open Mon through Fri, 9 a.m. to 5 p.m. It makes sense to have a flag maker in Philadelphia, right across from the home of legendary Betsy Ross. Although a talented seamstress, Ross has never been confirmed as the maker of the first US flag. But it's possible. First, Betsy did indeed make flags. Second, she was paid by the new country's navy for "making the ships colours." And she was paid a visit by a famous trio. In May or early June of 1776, Gen. George Washington; Robert Morris, the Pennsylvania delegate to the Continental Congress; and Col. George Ross, her late husband's uncle, were welcomed into her home. Ross, who may have recommended her for the job, gave Betsy a sketch of a flag for the new country, but she was never given credit for the flag and it was almost 100 years after the Revolutionary War that anyone made a claim on the origins for the flag. Either way, it's an established fact that Humphrys is originally from New York and started its business life as a manufacturer of sails back in 1805. In 1864, Humphrys came to Philly and is now one of the leaders in flag making. The shop is small and unassuming, but it's chock full of every kind of flag imaginable.

Pat's King of Steaks, MEAT, 1237 E. Passyunk Ave., Philadelphia 19147; (215) 468-1546; patskingofsteaks.com. Open 24 hours. The Philadelphia cheesesteak has become an iconic menu item all across America. The true cheesesteak sandwich has its origins in a small corner of Philadelphia—where it's still made and eaten. In 1930 Pat Oliveri (and brother Harry) opened a small hot dog stand at the base of the Italian Market. Deciding to do something different for lunch, he chopped some meat, removed the hot dog from its Italian roll, and replaced it with the meat. He dressed up his meat sandwich with some onions. A cab driver asked Pat to make him one like it as well. Forget the hot dogs, the cabbie declared, make these instead. And so he did. Per customer demand, cheese was almost immediately added. Pat's still sells hot dogs as well as pizza, fish cakes, french fries, and cheese fries. Pat's tongue-in-cheek attitude is apparent with the posted sign and online advice on "How to order like a local." You can order your cheesesteak "wit" or "wit-out" cheese. Over the past 80 years, Pat's has been visited by celebrities, presidents, actors, and athletes.

Philadelphia Soft Pretzel Company, PRETZELS, 4315 N. 3rd St., Philadelphia 19123; (215) 324-4315; philasoftpretzels.com. Open Mon through Fri, 5 to 11:30 a.m.; Sat, 6 to 10 a.m. In 1968 Dan Sidorick was an insurance salesman. He walked into a bakery and tried to sell the owner an insurance policy. He walked out with a delicious soft pretzel and an entire pretzel bakery. Turns out the owner wanted to get out of the business and sold the bakery to Dan on the spot. Since then, the Philadelphia Soft Pretzel Company has offered local folks something as soft and warm as a hug on a cold Pennsylvania day. Dan's son Joseph has taken over the family business and notes that when vendors first sold their soft pretzels on the street you could get two for a nickel. You can still buy them on the street, but expect to pay a bit more. The pretzels are ubiquitous in Philly and its environs. They show up almost everywhere, even in Philadelphia schools as snacks. The pretzels are available to order over the phone or online, but shipping isn't always a good choice. They're best eaten fresh and soft and warm.

Pollyodd, Naoj & Mot Distillery, DISTILLERY, 1908 E. Passyunk Ave.; Philadelphia 19148; (215) 271-1161; pollyodd.com. Open Wed through Fri, 4 to 9 p.m. *Dalle Mie Mani Al Tou Cuore* means "from my hands to your heart" in Italian. This is Joan Verratti's motto. As CEO and president of Naoj & Mot Distillery, she turned a hobby into an art. She opened this distillery (Naoj & Mot is Joan & Tom backwards) to make a business out of doing what she loves: making lemoncello. The Italian lemon-flavored liquor was famously introduced to an American audience in the movie *Under the Tuscan Sun*, in which Diane Lane is introduced to the sweet and strong lemony drink by the equally sweet and strong (and handsome)

Marcello. Joan creates artisan liquors, each containing no more than five locally sourced ingredients—water or cream, sugar, grain alcohol, fruit, or chocolate. And by the way, there's a Pollyodd Chocolatecello flavor—is your mouth watering yet? Currently, Joan offers a total of 10 different flavored "cellos," and she's hoping to expand the line. She donates a portion of her proceeds to fund a scholarship program in memory of her late son, Thomas. The Thomas Joseph Verratti, III Memorial Scholarship program helps defray cost for tuition at Philadelphia's Bishop Neumann High School.

Tasty Baking Company, FOOD/BAKERY, 4300 S. 26th St., Philadelphia 19112; (215) 221-8500 or (800) 248-2789; tastykake.com. Tastykake is the brand name for the line of cupcake-like sweet snacks made by the Tasty Baking Company. Krimpets, pies, and candy cakes have been eaten by residents, presidents, movie stars, and heads of state. Krimpets were originally finger-shaped cakes with a thick layer of icing, but when the bakers tried to pick up the cake it was so moist it fell apart between their fingers. Someone recommended that the bakers "crimp it." It worked, and so did the name. The individually wrapped snacks were just the right size to be the best part of lunch. Philip Bauer, cofounder of Tasty Baking Company, was born to bake. His father owned the Bauer Brothers Bakery in Pittsburgh, and young Philip eagerly learned the basics of snack making: great taste, good value, and, most importantly, fresh ingredients. When his father sold the Pittsburgh bakery, Philip joined forces with Herbert Morris, an egg salesman. They had the idea to individually wrap snack cakes and deliver them fresh daily. On February 25, 1914, with $50,000 they raised from family members, they founded Tasty Baking Company. Tastykakes were delivered daily by horse and wagon, and became a familiar sight on the streets of Philadelphia. The last horse was retired in 1941. In 2009 the Huntington Park bakery had seen its day. Tastykake settled on the Navy Yard in South Philadelphia and there they celebrated 100 years in a new bakery in 2014. But why Bauer spelled "cake" as "kake" is still a mystery. Tastykakes are available throughout the country. The company is now owned by Flowers Foods.

Wonder Bread, FOOD/BAKERY, 9801 Blue Grass Rd., Philadelphia 19114; (215) 969-1200; wonderbread.com. First conceived in 1921 by the Taggart Baking Company, Wonder Bread has grown into an iconic, pure white, nutrient-enriched loaf. Wonder Bread was the first to introduce the one-and-a-half-pound loaf, which was an advantage over the one-pounders that were being sold. In the 1930s, Wonder Bread was the first to the shelf with their sliced bread. But they had to weather a depression and two wars. From 1943 to 1945 just about all commercially baked bread was sold unsliced because of a steel shortage (steel slicers were in short supply) during World War II. But this bakery and bread, inspired by the "wonder" of the International Balloon Race at the Indianapolis Speedway and iconic balloon-shaped imagery, toughed it out with the rest of the country. They chugged through, making their Classic White Bread as well as hamburger and hot dog rolls. Later they added Whole Wheat Bread to their product line. After 90 years of baking, they've since scaled back. Their Hostess brand was shut down in 2009, but Wonder Bread can still be found on grocery shelves nationwide. They are now owned by Flowers Foods, the same company that owns Tastykakes.

Yards Brewing Company, BREWERY, 901 N. Delaware Ave., Philadelphia 19123; (215) 634-2600; yardsbrewing.com. Open daily, noon to p.m. Free brewery tours and tastings are offered on weekends from noon to 4 p.m. This brewery began life as a garage-size operation in the Manayunk section of Philadelphia, which is where their award-winning Extra

Special Ale was born. Since 1994 founder and brewmaster Tom Kehoe has upheld Yards' distinctive English-inspired style while continuing to embrace the innovative

spirit that defines American craft brewing. Ignore the irony of the colonies brewing English-styles ales. The American flair for a good brew is apparent in Yards' Ales of the Revolution. A true taste of history, these three beers are inspired by the original recipes of the founding fathers and fellow brewers George Washington, Thomas Jefferson, and Benjamin Franklin. You can also enjoy their Signature Ales, which include IPA, Brawler, Philadelphia Pale Ale, Love Stout, and ESA. Beyond those core favorites, their seasonal beers and limited releases keep things interesting throughout the year. The spacious bar area boasts friendly, knowledgeable staff, shuffleboard and pool tables, and an impressive view of the 9,000-square-foot brewhouse. Subtle touches like bar tops reconstructed from bowling lanes allude to the brewery's lasting commitment to craftsmanship and sustainability. Adding to their coolness, Yards is Pennsylvania's first 100 percent wind-powered brewery.

Potter

Brander Baskets, Hearts Desire, BASKETS, 27 W. Main St., Galeton 16922; (814) 435-2447 or (814) 435-2280; branderbaskets.com. Open Tues through Sat, 10 a.m. to 5 p.m.; Sun, noon to 3 p.m. Charlene Brander has been weaving baskets for over 15 years. She specializes in plain weave, antler, and rib baskets. What that means is that she uses discarded deer antlers (also called "sheds" since deer shed antlers every year) as handles instead of the typical reed or wood handles. Charlene also adorns her baskets with feathers and beads, which give the baskets a very unique and primitve aesthetic. Her ribbed baskets have rounded bottoms, which Charlene achieves by using hoops or ribs and weaving over them. These baskets come with or without handles. Her plain-weave baskets are structural and symmetrical with a tri-color lining. Her baskets have a warm, almost antique feel. But they're fresh and durable.

Firestone Forge, BLACKSMITH/GUNSMITH, 1280 Germania Rd., Galeton 16922; (814) 435-8277; firestoneforge.com. Hours vary, call prior to visit. Doug Firestone does the work of an 18th-century blacksmith. Not only in style and function but also in method and technique. Doug uses the similar hand tools and makes the same products that an early American blacksmith would have. Doug makes many of his own tools and does not use modern tools in his blacksmithing work. Doug is also a gunsmith, making historically accurate flintlock rifles and fowlers. He does historic demonstrations at select shows around the area. He has no problem working in front of an audience. He's used to people gathering around to watch him work. His interest in gunsmithing of early America (the Colonial era) actually led him into blacksmithing. While he pursues his love of iron, he's built flintlock guns in the process, sort of a consequence of his art. Doug and his family have been living in Potter County (also known as "God's Country" to the locals) for more than a decade. He enjoys making historically accurate 18th- and early 19th-century wares, tools, and hardware. Doug loves vistors, but between the road construction and the unpredictable Pennsylvania weather, he encourages visitors to call first for the best directions and times.

Schuylkill

Kepner Scott Shoe Co., APPAREL, 209 N. Liberty St., Orwigsburg 17961; (570) 366-0229; kepnerscott.com. Hours by appointment. The Kepner Scott Shoe Company is the oldest surviving children's shoe manufacturer in America. In 1888, in the town of Orwigsburg, Kepner Scott Shoe Co. was founded (a combination of the shoe firms of Haeseler, Kepner and Co., Alexander Scott, and W.C. Kepner). By 1913 the town was home to 11 shoe manufacturers, producing over a million pairs of children's shoes annually. As the years wore on, the children's shoe market was dominated by uncomfortable "welted" (stitched or glued to the sole) shoes. Former employee and new owner Milo Zimmerman believed children needed soft, flexible shoes. Because children's feet were tender and first steps tenuous, he felt children's shoes required cushiony soles and breathable upper materials. Milo and his son Clair decided to buck the trend and design healthier children's shoes. Creating their own last (shoe mold), they formulated shoes that supported the ankle and allowed the foot to move more freely. Clair assumed the leadership when his father passed away in 1982. Clair's children took over in 2000—representing the third generation of shoemakers. Kepner Scott Shoes are custom designed to fit little feet of all shapes and sizes. After 121 years, more than 10 million pairs of Kepner Scott shoes have been worn by children throughout the world.

Mrs. T's Pierogies, PIEROGIES, 600 E. Centre St., Shenandoah 17976; (800) PIEROGY; pierogies.com. Open Mon through Fri, 8 a.m. to 4:30 p.m. Atecco is the company that makes this Polish, traditionally potato-filled dumpling. It can be baked, boiled, or fried. The ethnic food is now a county fair favorite that joins the ranks of shoo-fly pie, funnel cakes, and dill pickles on a stick. It also appears as an appetizer or side dish in many eating establishments. Mary Twardzik and her original pierogy recipe were the inspiration for this successful business that began in 1952. Everybody in town, especially her son Ted, loved her pierogies. He spent his childhood watching, learning, and, of course, tasting these delights. After college, he spent a year working for an accounting firm before realizing this Polish specialty might have wider appeal. After all, if they did so well at church dinners, why wouldn't they be a favorite everywhere? Ted returned home to Shenandoah and started making pierogies in the very same kitchen where he had grown up watching his mother cook. Six weeks later, Mary asked him to move the mess elsewhere. Ted set up shop in his father's former tavern and began churning out pierogies by the dozen. Over the years, the company expanded to the surrounding buildings, but the tavern still remains a part of the Ateeco (which stands for "A, T for Twardzik, and Co for Company") headquarters. Today, Ted's son Tom is president of the company. Over 13 million pierogies in 14 different varieties leave Ateeco's kitchens every week. That's over half a billion pierogies a year. Mrs. T's Pierogies are distributed all across America, even to US military commissaries overseas.

Mud & Maker, FURNITURE, 6 South Centre St., Pottsville 17901; (484) 650-2745; mudandmaker.com. **Open Tues through Fri, noon to 7 p.m.** Ryan Zajac and Stephanie Premich get to do what they love—make things. Wood, pottery, you name it—if it involves their hands, they've got it going. Their wooden benches and tables are made under the Crowned Rabbit brand. Located in the historic district of downtown Pottsville (about 97 miles northwest of Philadelphia), their three-story brick-and-mortar building is filled with their work. The two love challenging each other to make one-of-kind thrown pottery pieces, (mugs and platters), small hand-sculpted pieces (magnets and coasters), as well as mixed media pieces. One line of hanging art resembles blossoming oyster shells. Both admit they are inspired by nature. They offer Wheel and Wine parties where adults can kick back, relax with a glass of BYOB wine, and get their hands muddy with clay. They also offer summer camps for kids. So their studio is like a spa and a training ground. Children develop their passions by being exposed to the hands-on process and technique of artwork, such as pottery. Even adults find themselves attracted to the artisanal journey of creating beautiful and functional pieces.

Rustic Turnings, WOODWORKING, Schuylkill Haven 17972; (570) 385-0248; rusticturnings.com. **Open by appointment only.** To say that Joseph Quesada kind of likes wood is like saying Popeye kind of likes spinach. Joseph has a passion for the feel and smell of wood that few people have, but one that everyone who sees his work understands. And yet, Joe's a late bloomer. For years, he patiently transported his wife to and from her craft shows. He frequently found himself in front of the wood turning tents, watching the masters (some younger than him), ply and teach their trade. Joe's turn at the woodworking life came after he took classes specifically centered around the woody technique. The hollowing out of stumps and pieces of wood involves two types of turning—one goes along the grain of wood (spindle turning), and the other is at different angles to the grain (bowl or faceplate turning). When wood is hollowed or cut against the grain, it sometimes tears, displaying holes and rough edges. It sounds awful, but when finished, it adds to the piece's uniqueness. Joe no longer watches at shows, he displays and sells his work. He has a small shop on his property, transforming ugly and forgotten pieces of wood into art so smooth and beguiling that your hands naturally reach for them.

Yuengling Brewery, BREWERY, 501 Mahantongo St., Pottsville 17901; (570) 622-4142; yuengling.com. Free tours usually offered Mon through Sat, 9 a.m. to 4 p.m., but times may change, so call first; gift shop and museum open Mon through Fri, 9 a.m. to 4 p.m.; Sat, 10 a.m. to 3 p.m. When a person changes their name, they don't change their personality. This applies to David Gottlob Jüngling, who immigrated to the US in 1823 and anglicized his real name Jüngling to Yuengling. When he began the Eagle Brewery in 1829, he changed nothing of his tenacity and ambition. In 1831 a large fire swept through the brewhouse, but David didn't quit, he rebuilt

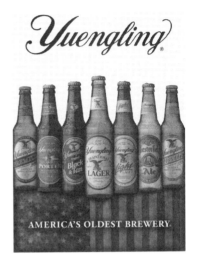

and kept brewing. In 1873 Eagle became Yuengling & Sons Brewery when David's son Frederick joined the business. Prohibition almost shut many US breweries down for good, but Yuengling kept on brewing, and innovating. The brewery continued to stay open by making "near beer," a low-alcohol (less than 1 percent alcohol by volume) beverage. Then the family tried their hand at dairy farming and made ice cream—success! It's still made to this day. While women in the beer industry currently represent only 10 percent of brewing jobs, current owner Richard Yuengling is further taking the lead in the industry. Three of his four daughters, Jennifer, Wendy, and Deborah, are getting ready to carry on the Yuengling tradition as the sixth generation of this Pennsylvanian brewing family.

Snyder

Selin's Grove Brewing Company, BREWERY, 121 Market St., Selinsgrove 17870; (570) 374-7308; selinsgrovebrewing.com. Open Wed through Thurs, 11:30 a.m. to 11 p.m.; Fri through Sat, 11:30 a.m. to midnight; Sun, 11:30 a.m. to 8 p.m. Technically the brewery opened in 1996. But the building it calls home was completed in 1816 by Pennsylvania's only three-term governor, Simon Snyder. Construction actually began in 1812, but the war with the British (again) halted the efforts. In the late 19th century, Matilda Pierce Alleman took up residence in the Snyder home. Alleman was famous for her autobiographical accounts of what she saw during the Civil War, most especially at Gettysburg. The building eventually had a distillery that went out of business. When you sip your Selin's Grove beer, you may notice there's a dog on the label. The owners heard historical accounts of how stray dogs were harnessed to run a large wheel to power the pumps that ran the old distillery. There were no animal protection acts in Selinsgrove back then. The owners wanted to pay respect to that dog power, so they placed a dog on their labels and every year they give to no-kill animal shelters. Selin's Grove also produces a rich and foamy root beer for non-beer drinkers. And for the courageous beer drinker, they offer a coffee stout—a dark beer infused with organic coffee that's so delicious it will make your morning java jealous.

Somerset

BumbleBerry Farms, HONEY, 124 Woodside Dr., Somerset 15501; (814) 279-8083; bumbleberryfarms.com. Call ahead for hours. Queen Bee should be the title on Karen Mosholder's business card. Karen is a beekeeper and honey-producer extraordinaire. She's a newbie to the bee business, only combing honey for about five years, but she loves what she does and doesn't mind the occasional sting. She dismisses it as an occupational hazard. Her motto, "spread a little sweetness on the planet," is also a mission statement. Her BumbleBerry Farms honey shop does just that. With the versatility that is quintessentially honey, she creates a wide spectrum of products from edible spreads to skin creams. Her line of honey-based cream spreads are sweet on everything from bread to poultry to your finger. True, bees are a rather dramatic way to begin any type of business, but Karen's entrepreneurial spirit and love of nature fuel her success. Yes, there are days when things get tough and she questions why she went the into buzzing business, but then something magical happens—a shout-out in a national magazine, or a request for her edibles from another country. She also has a comforting "hive" of support—family and friends who encourage and motivate her. And that gives her the validation that she's right where she should bee.

Tioga

Fay's Maple Products, MAPLE, 10640 Berwick Tpke., Columbia Cross Roads 16914; (570) 596-2816. Seasonal hours. At Fay's Maple Products, they produce, sell, and ship maple syrup, maple sugar, and maple cream. Duane Fay and his family have owned and operated their maple production facility since 1930. While maple syrup is always delicious any time of the year, the new health craze is Maple Water. Originally started in Vermont, a state that's practically synonymous with maple syrup, maple water is basically sap from the maple tree. Native Americans and North American explorers began tapping maple water hundreds of years ago. Early Americans and explorers couldn't safely drink the natural unfiltered, bacteria-contaminated water. If they did, they suffered from often-fatal bouts of dysentery or cholera. Hydrating with maple water (sap) was probably safer. The Fay family keeps it simple and untrendy and in March each year, hosts Pancake Days where breakfast is served all day and Fay's Maple syrup is poured out to profit community projects and needs. Pennsylvania is home to an abundant supply of all kinds of maple trees. But to make syrup, you use three species: sugar maple, black maple, or the red maple.

Glenfiddich Wool, KNITTING, 525 Dunkleberger Rd., Millerton 16936; (570) 549-5661; glenfiddichwool.net. Open Mon and Tues, 10 a.m. to 5 p.m., or by appointment. Thomas Jefferson would be jealous of Kathleen England—more specifically, of her flock of Border Leicester sheep. The signer of the Declaration of Independence raised his own flock for their merino wool. There were, however, unfortunate incidences of his rams harming several innocent passersby. Kathleen's sheep are docile and their wool prized by knitters and spinners because of its crimp and luster. Her family had been farming for decades but she established Glenfiddich Wool in 2002, with her knitting partner Barbara Condon. The whole wool infatuation began with their mutual love of fiber arts and knitting. Kathleen's husband Robby England, having grown up on a farm, comfortably shepherds (and sheers) a flock of over 150 sheep. The wool provides the perfect resource for Kathleen and Barbara's vision of custom-spun yarns. The business has since evolved to include hand dyeing, hand spinning, and custom designing patterns. In addition to being mindful of their impact on the environment and trying always to leave a small footprint, they have chickens and other livestock that sustain them. They do their best to teach their grandchildren about the origin of fabric. Their hope is to keep the farm and Glenfiddich Wool in the family.

Venango

Brown's Pure Maple Products, MAPLE, 1037 Carnes School Rd., Seneca 16346; (814) 437-9414; brownspuremaple.com. Jim and Darlene Brown and their family have been perfecting the art of sticky sweet, otherwise known as the fine art of making 100 percent pure maple syrup. It's been a long-standing tradition in the Brown family. For five generations, the Brown's have been tapping into northwest Pennsylvania's abundance of maple trees and producing a high-quality, pure maple syrup along with a line of pure maple products. A family-owned and -operated business, Brown's Pure Maple started out as a hobby and has grown into a full-time operation. Jim Brown started making maple syrup at the age of 10 with his father. He has continued this tradition with his own children and grandchildren. Today Brown's is owned and operated by Jim Brown, his son Doug Brown, and his daughter Kim Shaffer. Jim's wife Darlene is also a vital part of the day-to-day operations with her skill and creativity in the test kitchen. Darlene is the inspiration behind all of the new products. Her recipes and innovative uses of their pure maple products can be found on their Brown's Recipe Blog. Their products are available online and at local farmers' markets.

Warren

Main Street Artisan's Co-op, GENERAL ARTISANS, 31 South Main St., Sheffield 16347; (814) 968-5596; mainstreetartisansco-op.com/artisans/janicelyle. Open 11 a.m. to 5 p.m. Janice Lyle is a self-taught braider, using reclaimed and new wool fabrics. She's been retired from social services, but has always enjoyed making things, ever since she was little. Like most moms, she became all about domestic arts sewing, refinishing and refurbishing in order to stretch, ahem, manage the family budget. About eight years ago she discovered a book on crafting items using weaving and braiding techniques. She now makes rugs, tablemats, and runners. The curious and crafty mom that she is, she's not afraid to experiment with baskets, and five-strand braids. She hand-braids and crochets the lace for a finished product that will last for many years, combining function with beauty. She puts her spin on her handmade artistry with her more up-to-date choices and combinations of colors and textures. Her favorite fabric to work with is wool. She says it's durable, washable, nearly stain resistant, comes in an abundance of colors, and has a lovely feel to it. And it's mom-approved. Her creations can be found at the Main Street Artisan's Co-op in Sheffield.

Old Iron Forge, IRONWORKS, 33 Mason Rd., Warren 16365; (814) 730-8856; oldironforge.com. Open Mon through Sat, 7 a.m. to 5 p.m. Michael Covell has lived all over the US, but there's something about the Allegheny Forest, mountain laurel, and an iron forge that keeps him in one place. It's a Pennsylvania thing. Michael has been pounding iron into beautifully intricate shapes in Warren County for about 15 years. His work has adorned gates, stairways, and windows in California, Arizona, and Florida. He's always had irons in the fire, so to speak, and is happy to say that his son Jordan Michael also loves the rugged art. In a state that has towns with names like Steelton, Ironton, and Old Forge, it's no surprise the people of Pennsylvania and metal are eternally welded together. Although steel mills are closing, the art of metalwork hasn't quite disappeared. There's a resurgence of the love of the hand-forged. Open-die, or smith forging, requires the iron to be heated (to almost 2000°F), which softens it. It is then hammered into the desired shape or thickness. Or pieces may be joined together using the same method. Imagine, then, using this technique to make an entire spiral staircase, or a gate to span a driveway. As hot and dirty as the creative process sounds, Covell's results are nothing short of breathtaking.

Washington

All-Clad, METALWORKS, 424 Morganza Rd., Canonsburg 15315; (800) 255-2523; all-clad.com. In 1967 Clad Metals began as a small metalworks plant specializing in forming bonded metals for a variety of companies. Metallurgist John Ulam recognized that the combination of different metals yielded composites with superior heating results. He went on to develop 60 patents for bonded metals. One of the more successful All-Clad pans is the bonding of steel to an aluminum core. Like a metal sandwich, providing the heat conduction of aluminum and the durability of steel, these pots and pans marry the best qualities of two metals. Ulam established All-Clad Metal Crafters in 1971 and began producing professional-quality cookware for working chefs and avid home cooks. Ulam made sure he used American-made steel. The company makes cutlery, tools, and electronic appliances that appear in the William Sonoma and Bed, Bath & Beyond catalogs. Hint: For all you newlyweds-to-be, one of these pots, pans, or accessories is something you'll want to put on your bridal registry.

Bedillion Honey Farm, HONEY, 1179 Burgettstown Rd., Hickory 15340; (724) 356-7713; bedillionhoneyfarm.com. Hours are seasonal, so it's best to call ahead. Sara and Mark Bedillion are all about the buzz. The healthy, busy kind that produces liquid gold. Their adventure with bees started in June 2004 with one hive of bees. It soon turned into two hives, then ten, then twenty, and now over one hundred! With some care and a little luck, come spring, those hives turn into more. Not all honeybees are alike. The type of honeybees Bedillion keeps are survivor stock of mainly Italian and some Russian honeybees. They have proven to be gentle, hygenic, and good producers of brood and honey. During their farm market's open season, from around May to October, you can buy seasonal produce and fruit. And you can see some of the honeybees up close in an observation beehive right in the market. You can watch the workers bringing in pollen on their legs, watch the queen lay eggs, and even watch the bees dance.

Channel Craft Toys, TOYS AND GAMES, P.O. Box 101, North Charleroi 15022; (724) 489-4900; channelcraft.com. Channel Craft began as a one-man operation in 1983 from the back of a traveling wood shop, which was actually a van in disguise. President and founder Dean Helfer, Jr. drove from craft shows to folk festivals peddling his handcrafted wooden products. The craft circuit opened new avenues and provided the necessary cash flow to put together a true manufacturing operation. Finally Dean and his crew settled in the small mining town of Ellsworth to set up a "permanent" shop to handcraft wooden toys. Dean had rubbed elbows with many other US toy and game manufacturers and had worked out distributor partnerships to sell their products along with the Channel Craft toys. Space constraints required Channel Craft to seek out a larger manufacturing facility in order to continue producing. In 1991 Dean and Channel Craft settled into an old Army Corps of Engineers building south of Pittsburgh on the banks of the Monongahela River in Charleroi. There, with 70 employees, Channel Craft made toys, games, and puzzles for thousands of museums, specialty toy and gift shops, mail-order catalog companies, and department stores. With an addition of a new warehouse and shipping facility in 1998, Channel Craft and Dean expanded. They currently occupy three buildings—for manufacturing, assembly, and shipping/receiving—and continue to handcraft toys, games, and puzzles. Each year, new products grace the pages of their catalog and online store. You'll probably never find Channel Craft products in the major discount stores or worldwide superstore chains.

The Glass Place, GLASS, 531 Georgetown Rd., Lawrence 15055; (724) 969-0575; theglassplace.com. Open Tues through Fri, 10 a.m. to 5 p.m.; Sat, 10 a.m. to 3 p.m. Ruth Mahoney doesn't necessarily need to see through glass. In fact, for this artisan it's better if she can't. She prefers color. Lots of color. And when the sunlight beams through—it's all good. Ruth didn't always look at glass as an artistic medium. Her sister bought classes in glasswork as a gift for both of them. Ruth fell in love with it, while her sister just didn't feel as enthused. Often stained glass is associated with churches, chapels, or other ecclesiastical settings, but there's no end to the pieces that can be created. Homes or businesses can be fitted with their own stained glass windows (think company logo). Stained glass can be used to make Tiffany or pendant lamps, custom transoms, trays, frames, jewelry, and more. Ruth also creates fused glass pieces. The glass is layered and heated in a kiln to "melt" into a mold. Her store sells supplies for the glass crafter. And if something breaks, she's there to help repair it. It's been over 25 years since Ruth and her sister took a stained glass class together. Ruth has filled her sister's house with all sorts of stained glass art. They have both benefited from her passion.

Sarris Candies, CANDY/CHOCOLATE, 511 Adams Ave., Canonsburg 15317; (800) 255-7771; sarriscandies.com. Open Mon through Sat, 9 a.m. to 9 p.m.; Sun, 10 a.m. to 9 p.m. Athena Sarris Sims of Sarris Candies isn't your average candymaker (as if there were such a thing). Her company goes above and beyond chocolate-coated confections and tempting treats—they also make ice cream. If it's not making you smile, melting in your mouth, or dripping down your chin—she's not going to sell it. It started with her dad Frank Sarris. As a young man trying to win over his sweetheart, Frank presented the object of his affections with a box of chocolates. Her face lit up as she lifted the lid. Frank knew he was in love. He also knew he could make better chocolates. Soon, Frank and his sweetheart were married. At first he began producing small amounts of candy in his basement for friends and family. Working as a forklift operator by day and candymaker by night, Frank was torn. He took a chance and quit his forklift job and started stirring batches full time. By 1963 Frank had outgrown his basement and built a small candy shop. Five years later, an even bigger candy shop was built. Frank never forgot the soda fountains of his youth, which sold ice cream and penny candy. In 1982 with the help of his son, he created an old-fashioned ice cream parlor complete with period-style red and brass booths and shimmering crystal chandeliers. It sounds like a Willy Wonka dream. The Sarris Chocolate Factory and Ice Cream Parlour fill an area the size of a football field with over 100 yards of chocolate, penny candy, ice cream, and toys. Thousands of people visit annually to sample Sarris's homemade ice cream, sundaes (with all the custom toppings), and other treats.

Wayne

Calkins Creamery, DAIRY, 288 Calkins Rd., Honesdale 18431; (570) 729-8103; calkinscreamery.com. Hours are seasonal, so it's best to call ahead to confirm. Here's the equation: Grass + cows + culture + cave = amazing cheese. And yes, the mathematic probability bears it out. The sum of ingredients and a touch of playful experimentation make the creamery on the Highland Farm unique among creameries in Pennsylvania. And with names like Vampire Slayer, Old Man Highlander, and Horsekick, you know this is not ordinary cheese. But then Emily and Jay Montgomery aren't ordinary farmers making a living off of all things cheesy. Sure, they love the land, but they also love keeping it local by using Pennsylvania beer to make curds for their Gouda (rumor has it they're using Yuengling Porter). Highland Farm was originally established by Burton and Elizabeth Bryant in 1841, and it took some ingenuity and a lot of hard work to turn the farm (and a cave) into the successful cheese business it is today. Their cheeses can be found in four states and DC. Making cheese isn't a desk job—you can't just expect milk to naturally progress into creamy curds all by itself. You need to stir and check on it frequently. Even aged cheese (cheddar can age up to a year or more) needs a little extra love. So the lucky cows at Highland farms receive some serious TLC even before they give milk.

Thomas Fishing Lures, SPORTING EQUIPMENT, 316 Wayne Ave., Hawley 18428; (570) 226-4011 or (800) 724-6768; thomaslures.com. In 1938, an apprentice tool and die maker from Czechoslovakia, Richard Shubert, came to America with a dream of producing fishing lures. Knowing her son needed to learn to communicate in the more than one language, she sent him to a relative in Montana to be tutored in English. The rivers and lakes of Montana and the surrounding Rocky Mountain region provided the perfect setting to test his prototypes and market his innovative new lures to customers. During the mid-1940s he returned to family in New York City, and the young entrepreneur began producing Thomas Spinning Lures in a small shop on Manhattan's lower east side. For the next 15 years, with the popularity of spin-fishing growing rapidly, so did the popularity of Thomas's unique line of spoons and spinners, with sales eventually expanding into many other famous trout fishing areas of the US. While vacationing at Lake Wallenpaupack in the late 1950s, Richard discovered the tranquil beauty of the Pocono Mountains region and decided to move his thriving business to northeastern Pennsylvania. In 1961 Thomas Lures began manufacturing fishing lures in Hawley, Pennsylvania, where it continues to operate to this day. In fact, they've been working in the same buildings for more than 50 years. They have a handful of employees dedicated to providing American-made, high-quality fishing lures at reasonable prices. Call or go online for a catalog of their merchandise.

Westmorland

Gosia's Pierogies, PIEROGIES, 75 Pauline Dr., Latrobe 15650; (724) 205-9938; **gosiaspierogies.com. Open Mon through Fri, 9 a.m. to 5 p.m.** These pierogies are homemade and handmade using the best ingredients. Gosia's pierogi recipe came from Poland to the US (via Canada). Owners Jan and Terry Rawecki turned their love of this very ethnic dumpling into a successful business. Each pierogie is cooked immediately after it is formed and stuffed. Once cooked, the pierogie is air-cooled and packaged fresh. Then the pierogie packs are sealed, labeled, and stored to lock in the fresh flavor. In a similar setup to a deli, customers go into Gosia's and order pierogis to go, or pick orders called in ahead of time. They offer seven fillings— potato and cheese, cabbage (sweet), sauerkraut, sweet poato, prune, cottage cheese, and chicken. Pierogies are a staple at nearly every Pennsylvania county fair and festival. Though a simple dish, making pierogies isn't that easy. The dough can be made with or without eggs. If you use eggs, the dough will remain rigid. Leaving out the eggs yields a soft dough, but it can fall apart if you're not careful. Hint: For best results, don't boil your frozen Gosia's pierogies. Thaw, then sauté for a few minutes on each side. During the weekends, Jan and Terry offer their pierogies at local food festivals and farmers' markets thoroughout the Pittsburgh area. Check their website for a complete list of locations.

Luna Jaze, LEATHER, Pittsburgh 15232; (412) 512-7468; lunajaze@yahoo .com; lunajaze.com.) When Jamie Murphy heard, "No, I can't fix it," from her local shoe repair man, she wasn't dismayed, she took it as a challenge. She repaired her beloved leather bag on her languishing sewing machine. Then she thought, I can make one of my own. And so she did. Now, most women do not give away their purses unless someone is pointing a weapon at their heart, but give away her purse, she did. In an office supply store, a gentleman insisted his girlfriend would love Jamie's newly created leather purse. Even the price didn't deter him—$300. Sold! And thus began Luna Jaze. Each work begins as an artistic dance. She allows her Italian leather to lead. The piece introduces itself, coyly revealing its imperfections, flaws any other leather worker would immediately discard. But Jamie allows the imperfections of the leather to shine. In her artist's eye, she sees the uniqueness and transforms the once ugly into beautiful. Yes, Jamie has cool pictures of her yummy leather bags, attachés, and clutches on her Etsy site. And, oh yeah, she was an entrant in Martha Stewart Made in America for her creations. But her happiest moment thus far was when she saw someone wearing her bag. It was like someone was singing her song. Jamie's work is more than just an accessory, but is offered at the prestigious Pittsburgh Center for the Arts (6300 Fifth Ave., Pittsburgh 15232; 412-361-0873. Open Tue through Fri, 10 a.m. to 5 p.m.; Sat, 10 a.m. to 3 p.m.; Sun, noon to 4 p.m.).

Wyoming

Sassy Albert Soaps, SOAP, 35 East Tioga St., Tunkhannock 18657; (570) 606-4107; sassyalbertsoap.com. **Open Mon through Sat, 11 a.m. to 4 p.m.** In 1991 Michael Wisosky inherited his family's small farm. He always kept various handmade soaps, bought at local craft fairs and vacations that he took, available because he had a hard time remembering birthdays and anniversaries and for the occasional hostess gift. On a trip to London, he bought a bar of specialty soap for $18. The sticker shock made him wonder, *why not make my own?* He thought that soapmaking must be like cooking, and he had been working as a chef for most of his adult life. He knew the secret to creating something special is hard work, knowledge, and loving what you are doing, so he decided to venture into the soapmaking business. Through trial and error, classes, and chemistry, he learned the art. Now, instead of steaming vegetables, he gathers herbs and distills them. He's an "evolving soapmaker" and continuously improves the quality of his handmade, all-natural products. All of Sassy Albert's soaps contain jojoba oil because it does for wonders for the skin. He assures his customers that once you use the oil, nothing else measures up. The name Sassy Albert comes from two Scottish terriers who own him—people don't own terriers, it's the other way around. They're the driving force of the company and a fixture in the store. Gift-giving hint: A sample of Sassy Albert's handmade soaps are perfect presents for just about any occasion.

York

Family Heirloom Weavers, TEXTILES, 775 Meadowview Dr., Red Lion 17356; (717) 873-6134; familyheirloomweavers.com. **Tours available the last Sat of each month.** Family Heirloom is one of the last mills of textiles and fabric in the US. The cool thing about this company is that they use vintage looms from the 1930s and '40s, shuttle looms, looms that make center seams, a warping wheel, and creel. The whole place is one big loom, churning out woven textiles. Each weaver has his or her name listed next to textile, an artist getting credit for his or her work. The not-so-cool thing is that it takes time to produce the textiles. The looms are still in need of hands-on management. Their Traditional and French Country collections are a Colonial-style decorator's dream. Their carpets and rugs are sold through the gracious Winterthur Museum's House of Style (located in Delaware). Unfortunately their textiles are copied or knocked off, and it leads to unfair price competition. Their customers are aware of it and know that quality isn't cheap. Family Heirloom Weavers truly believe they are making heirlooms—something beautiful, durable, and not made in China. The Show House and Mill are open for tours for those 12 and older. Please call ahead to schedule.

Martin's Potato Chips, POTATO CHIPS, 5847 Lincoln Hwy. West, Thomasville 17364; (717) 792-3565; martinschips.com. Tours offered Tues at 9, 10, and 11 a.m. only. Reservations required. In 1941, a unique potato chip was created in the farm kitchen of Harry and Fairy Martin. The chip found its way into the hearts and homes of the residents surrounding their farm. Demand soon outgrew the kitchen. The Martins built a small factory and expanded their distribution from delivering fresh daily to market stands, to selling to mom-and-pop

grocery stores. In 1971 the business was sold to Ken and Sandy Potter, but the Martins stayed on as employees. The Potters dreamed of expanding the business outside the York area. By 1977 the delivery routes increased from one to five, covering York, Lancaster, Dauphin, and Adams Counties. Today over 60 routes operate from the distribution facilities in Thomasville, Reading, Allentown, Milton, and Lancaster (and even in Maryland) to ensure products are delivered fresh daily. They also serve bigger cities such as Pittsburgh, Philadelphia, Scranton, as well as the states of New York, New Jersey, Virginia, and West Virginia. In 2004, Ken, Jr. took over as president and CEO when Ken, Sr. retired. Martin's chips are superbly crunchy and have a homemade taste that's refreshing in comparison to the mass-produced limp snacks. They also distribute a full line of snack products. All potato chips and popcorn are made in their 80,000-square-foot Thomasville facility, which produces more than one million bags each month.

Snyder's of Hanover, Inc., PRETZELS, 1350 York St., Hanover 17331; (717) 632-4477; snydersofhanover.com. Open Mon through Fri, 9 a.m. to 6 p.m. The crunchy pretzels, also known as hard pretzels, began their journey to your snack bowl around the 1500s in Europe. One monk (whose name has been lost to time) had a reputation for playing with scraps of dough, tying them into knots before baking them. One of his brethren saw his knots and remarked that it looked like children praying, arms crossed against their chests. The Latin name *pretiola*, which means "little rewards," evolved into the word *pretzel*. In 1909 parent company, Hanover Canning Company, was founded and began producing Old Tyme Pretzels. In the 1920s, Eda and Edward Snyder made potato chips in their kitchen and sold them to local stores. The Snyder family united in business and, with Old Tyme Pretzels and Grandma Snyder's Chips, grew their brand name. The simple technology of aluminum foil bags in the 1940s kept pretzels from going stale and increased the shelf life and, consequently, the shipping range of Snyder's snacks. The company now bakes and ships its snacks from Pennsylvania internationally. Snyder's merged with Lance Food Company (Snyder's-Lance) in 2010, and is now one of the largest snack food companies in the country. Tours (with free samples) are available (large groups should call ahead) and there is an outlet store on premise.

Utz Quality Foods, PRETZELS/POTATO CHIPS, 900 High St., Hanover 17331; (800) 367-7629; utzsnacks.com. Self-guided factory tours are available Mon through Thurs, 9 a.m. to 4 p.m., please call first to confirm hours. The Utz story begins in a small town kitchen in 1921. William (Bill) and Salie Utz began producing

Hanover Home Brand Potato Chips in their summer kitchen, cooking about 50 pounds of chips an hour. They sold their fresh chips to small local grocers and markets, originally in the Baltimore, Maryland, area, before expanding. In 1930, to meet a growing demand for their snacks, the first section of the Utz plant was built on McAlister Street in Hanover, the rear of Bill and Salie Utz's home. A new manufacturing facility was later built there in 1938 and after World War II, Utz built a new 10-acre facility in Hanover. As Utz continued to expand geographically and consumer demand grew, they expanded with the addition of two more facilities in the 1970s. By this time, they had added pretzels to their product line. And, as time went on and consumer wants and needs continued to evolve, Utz went online, giving customers more access to purchase snacks from just about anywhere. Today Utz stands 94 years young and remains a privately owned and family-managed company based in Hanover. The company produces a full line of snack products, including potato chips, pretzels, cheese snacks, corn products, veggie snacks, and popcorn. Utz has manufacturing facilities located across Pennsylvania, along with additional facilities in Louisiana, California, Colorado, and Massachusetts. Utz Quality Foods, Inc. products are distributed nationally through grocery, mass-merchant, club stores, convenience stores, drug stores, and other channels under the Utz, Zapp's Potato Chips, Dirty Chips Potato Chips, Good Health, Bachman, and Wachusett's brands.

Index